Alexander Hamilton Wingfield

Poems and Songs

In Scotch and English

Alexander Hamilton Wingfield

Poems and Songs
In Scotch and English

ISBN/EAN: 9783744714211

Printed in Europe, USA, Canada, Australia, Japan

Cover: Foto ©Thomas Meinert / pixelio.de

More available books at **www.hansebooks.com**

POEMS AND SONGS,

IN

Scotch and English,

BY

ALEX. H. WINGFIELD.

Oh, Canada ! I lo'e ye weel !
Altho' nae son o' thine,
Within thy wide domain there beats
Nae truer heart than mine.

HAMILTON, ONT.

1873.

PRINTED AT THE "TIMES" BOOK AND JOB OFFICE.

TO

𝕵𝖔𝖘𝖊𝖕𝖍 𝕻𝖗𝖎𝖈𝖊, 𝕰𝖘𝖖., 𝕲𝖊𝖓𝖊𝖗𝖆𝖑 𝕸𝖆𝖓𝖆𝖌𝖊𝖗, 𝕲.𝖂.𝕽.,

HAMILTON,

THIS BOOK

IS

RESPECTFULLY DEDICATED

BY

THE AUTHOR.

CONTENTS.

xiv   CONTENTS.

MISCELLANEOUS.

SONGS.

PREFACE.

In these days the notion prevails that poetry, like miracles, has ceased, and it requires a certain amount of courage for an individual unknown to fame to come forward and say, varying the memorable expression of a great painter, that he, too, is a poet. This is the age not only of mechanical invention, supposed to be the very antithesis of poetry, but— more dreadful still—of criticism; the terrors of which make timorous poets pause. Homer and Milton stood in no dread of reviewers; though, to do justice to our own time, it must be added that they were at certain disadvantages for want of publishers! We are most of us half conscious of a belief that poetry was to be looked for as a matter of course in days gone by, when shepherds piped by the banks of classic streams, and when scholars assembled in academic groves; or when, in more recent times, our own poets found inspiration by lake and mountain, around some—

"Sweet Auburn, loveliest village of the plain,"

or in meditative quiet and solemn stillness of the

country churchyard. But can poetry be born amid
the noisy rattle of the loom, the birr of wheels,
the clang of hammers, the screaming whistle and
thundering rush of the locomotive? The possi-
bility of such a thing is perhaps barely admitted, but
we all put it among things unexpected and not likely
to happen.

However, out of the nettle danger may be plucked
the flower safety sometimes; and the writer of the
following unpretending collection thinks that his
own is a case in point. In the newspaper press—
the result and representative of what steam, the
telegraph, and mechanical invention generally can
achieve, the office of which, along with that of giving
news, is criticism—he has found the bridge that has
carried him where otherwise, perhaps, he would not
have ventured. Had it been proposed to him some
years ago to come before the public with a book—
actually a book—he would have thought that an
experiment was being made on his simplicity. But,
pushing out, as it were, his little boat now and then,
and always keeping near shore, he finds himself at
last induced to make a larger venture. Giving his
verses to the public at intervals for a number of
years past, through the medium of the newspaper
press, the public so favorably received them that he
was encouraged to keep on. And so it comes to
pass that in the joint result and triumph of two

supposed anti-poetical powers, that of mechanics and criticism together—the newspaper press—the poet finds, if not the wings to fly aloft with, at least the medium in which he may more easily bear himself up. The press gave the opportunity, the public have given a most encouraging measure of approval, and the author invites the public to consider themselves in no small degree responsible for the appearance of this little volume.

One merit the author is bold to claim, that of sincerity. He ventures to say, with Robert Nicoll—too early lost to the world—that he has written his *heart* in his poems ; and that "rude, unfinished, and hasty as they are, it can be read there." As he has really felt, or believed, or imagined, so has he written ; and, whatever faults of expression there may be in his efforts, there is no failure in honesty of intention. Having neither read much nor travelled far, nor been able to put the world of nature and of history under contribution, he has found his subjects chiefly among the familiar scenes and every-day experiences of his own humble walk in life ; taking such colour and impression of them as residence in a busy commercial and manufacturing city like Hamilton could not fail to present. Most of his lines have been struck out amid the din of the Great Western boiler shop, during working hours, and have been committed to paper in the evening, after the labours of the day were over. If there be poetry in them at all, it is such as comes from homely, natural inspiration, unaided either by varied reading or literary leisure.

Many of the pieces are written in the Lowland Scottish dialect, the author's mother tongue, which abounds with words having no exact equivalent in the English of the present day—words that, within a certain range of subjects, add much to the poet's resources of rhyme and expression. And such English as the poet uses is the plain, popular Saxon speech, unmixed with long words of learned derivation. If the public give no worse welcome to this collection than they have generally given to the author's pieces, as they appeared singly, he will consider himself to have been favourably judged and well received.

HAMILTON, CANADA, Sept., 1873.

POEMS AND SONGS

BY

A. H. WINGFIELD.

The Queen.

OUR QUEEN, our guid and gracious Queen,
　Lang may she live and reign !
For lang it may be e'er we ha'e
　The like o' her again.
God send her mony happy days—
　As mony as she's seen,
And ilka ane bring peace and joy
　To our beloved Queen.

Few names are mair revered than hers,
　And few deserve to be,
For there is nane that's filled her place
　Frae fau'ts has been sae free.
To a' that's wrang she's been a foe—
　To a' that's richt a frien',
And Britain canna boast a gem
　Mair bright than Britain's Queen.

A virtuous lassie in her youth,
    And later in her life,
She proved to ane that lo'ed her weel
    A guid and faithfu' wife ;
And to her subjects ane and a'
    A mither she has been—
She shares our joys and shares our griefs,
    Our leal, true-hearted Queen.

The page o' history ye may scan,
    But canna find her peer,
Nor ane that's lo'ed her people wi'
    A love that's mair sincere ;
And history will record her yet
    As ane o' royal blood
That weel has earned the title of
    " VICTORIA THE GOOD."

The Land That's Truly Free.

AULD SCOTIA'S BARDS in praises sing
O' hills and heather bells,
O' linns gaun loupin doon their glens
Whaur bonnie lassies dwells ;
And weel I loe that land mysel',
Wi' a' its ancient fame,
For whaur's the Scot whose heart ne'er warms
Whene'er he thinks o' hame ?
But there's anither land I trow
That's just as dear to me—
'Tis Canada, the only land
Whose sons are truly free.

The Saxon minstrels proudly sing
O' deeds their sons hae done,
And vaunt of a' their works of art,
And battle fields they've won ;
But can they boast a land like ours,
Whaur peace and plenty smile,
And labor sheds its blessings aye
On a' our sons o' toil ?
Na, na, though Englishmen are great,
They're no sae blest as we
In Canada, the only land
On earth that's truly free.

Auld Erin's Harp has aft been struck
  In wailin' tones o' grief,
But here her sons are prosperin'
  Beneath the Maple Leaf ;
And tho' nae dout they think at times
  On glories passed awa,
The sun shines bricht in Canada
  Alike on ane and a' ;
And as they hae been in the past,
  Sae will their future be,
In Canada, the only land
  Whose sons are truly free.

Let English, Irish, Scotch and French,
  Thegither here combine,
To emulate the deeds their sires
  Hae done in auld lang syne ;
We'll lay their failin's a' aside,
  Their virtues we'll retain,
And in our new Dominion they
  Will bring forth fruit again ;
And if our fathers loved their land
  As dearly, so will we
Love Canada, the only land
  On earth that's truly free.

Though young yet in the warld's affairs,
  And maybe kind o' blate,
We may excel our mither yet
  In a' that's guid and great ;

When speakin' o' her dawtit bairn
    She'll say o' us wi' pride,
There's no a land like Canada
    In a' creation wide.
Then swell the anthem loud and lang,
    And let your pæns be
‾To Canada, dear Canada,   .
    The glorious and the free.

A Shillin' or Twa.

FRIEN'SHIP has charms for the leal an' the true,
There's but few things can beat it the hale warld thro',
But you'll gey aften find that the best frien' ava
Is that white-headed callan' a shillin' or twa.
Eh, man, it's a fine thing, a shillin' or twa ;
Hech, man, it's a gran' thing, a shillin' or twa.
It keeps up your spirits, it adds to your merits,
If ye but inherit a shillin' or twa.

It's surprisin' how much you'll be thocht o' by men,
You'll get credit for wisdom altho' ye hae nane ;
You may be but a dunce yet be honor'd by a'
When they ken that ye hae a bit shillin' or twa.
Eh, man, it's a fine thing, a shillin' or twa ;
Hech, man, it's a gran' thing, a shillin or twa.
You'll ne'er ken what it means to want plenty o' frien's,
Gin ye glamor their een wi' a shillin' or twa.

But it alters the case when your siller's a' dune,
Then your frien's seem to gang a' awa wi' the win',
There's naebody then likes to ken you ava
When ye ask for the lend o' a shillin' or twa.
Eh, man, it's a fine thing, a shillin' or twa ;

Hech, man, it's a gran' thing, a shillin' or twa.
But there's no mony then that will haud out their han'
And say, tak' this, my man, there's a shillin' or twa.

A tocherless lass, tho' o' guid pedigree,
May ne'er hae a lover her mou' for to pree,
But let her get riches and sweethearts will fa'
Around her in dizens for her shillin' or twa.
Eh, man, it's a fine thing, a shillin' or twa;
Hech, man, it's a gran' thing, a shillin' or twa.
But it adds a new grace to each charm in her face
Gin her purse in it's place hauds a shillin' or twa.

Politicians will tell you that the country they "save,"
And wi' eloquence burning, they rant and they rave,
But at the year's end, when their salary they draw,
They aye save themsel's a bit shillin' or twa.
Eh, man, it's a fine thing, a shillin' or twa;
Hech, man, it's a gran' thing, a shillin' or twa.
They whiles do their best when they're put to the test,
But they feather their nest wi' a shillin' or twa.

Some folks fecht for siller year out and year in,
There are ithers that cheat for't, and ne'er think't a sin,
And there's some sae devoid o' morality's law,
Wud shake han's wi' the de'il for a shillin' or twa.
Eh, man, it's a fine thing, a shillin' or twa;
Hech, man, it's a gran' thing, a shillin' or twa :
To become rich and great, and hae flunkeys to wait
When you drive out in state, aff your shillin' or twa.

But we scorn the fause loon, that for vain warldly pelf,
Wud wrang ither folk to get riches himself;
" Aye live and let live," and deal justly by a',
And may you ne'er want for a shillin' or twa.
Eh, man, it's a fine thing, a shillin' or twa ;
Hech, man, it's a gran' thing, a shillin' or twa.
When you've wealth in your store, aye remember the poor,
And blessin's will shower on your shillin' or twa.

Ne'er Talk Lightly o' a Woman.

NE'ER talk lightly o' a woman,
  Though she whiles may gang astray,
Till ye ken how much temptation
  Has been thrown within her way ;
Ask yoursel' could ye withstood it,
  If the cause had been the same—
Ten to ane but you will answer
  That she isna much to blame.

Nae doubt but there's kittle kimmers
  That you'll meet wi' now and then,
But the maist o' them are better
  Than the common run o' men ;
Though we're tauld that woman brought us
  Sorrow wi' a vengeance ance,
Weel ken I mankind has wrought her
  Plenty sorrow for it since.

They wha glibly talk o' women
  Aften are the very anes
That have wranged them and abused them—
  Been the cause o' a' their sins ;
Wretches that have got nae feeling—
  For theirsel's they live and move—
May they never ken the pleasures
  O' an honest woman's love.

Ye wha lightly talk o' women,
  Aye keep mind there's ane or twa
That ye never want to hear them
  Lightly spoken o' ava :
Whaur's the man but thinks his mither
  Was as guid as needs to be ?
What's the reason, then, that ithers
  Shouldna hae as good as he ?

Would ye learn the worth o' women,
  Tak' a guid ane to yoursel',
Then you'll find out a' their virtues—
  Mair o' them than I can tell ;
Canada has plenty o' them—
  Lovesome lassies trig an' braw,
Just as guid an' just as bonnie
  As the wide world ever saw.

Wale a guid ane frae amang them,
  Cherish her wi' love an' care,
An' my word for't, that you'll never
  Lightly speak o' women mair.
Do this and you're sure to prosper—
  De'il confound the lang-tongued loon
Wha tak's either pride or pleasure
  Tryin' to rin women doon.

It's Best to Ha'e Ceevility.

It's best to ha'e ceevility,
  It always answers weel,
The auld wife said ae mornin',
  When she curchied to the deil ;
But though it may be richt at times
  To gi'e Auld Nick his due,
Ye maun tak' care he disna get
  A mortgage upon you.

It's guid to ha'e a ceevil tongue,
  Whatever else you ha'e—
It's like a passport in your pouch
  Whaure'er you chance to gae ;
Men greet ye when ye pass them by,
  And always wish you weel,
And say—as soon's your out o' sicht—
  There gangs a decent cheil.

It disna do to gang aroun'
  As surly as a bear,
And girn and growl the hale day lang,
  And fret, and fume, and swear ;
And keep folks in hot water wi'
  Your everlasting din—

That's no the way to gain respect,
Nor men's esteem to win.

Ye maun be courteous and kind,
And ne'er give way to strife,
For angry words ha'e got an edge
As keen and sharp's a knife.
Ne'er mak' an enemy o' ane
That ye can mak' your frien'—
Sow kindness, and you may be sure
That kindness you will glean.

Ne'er be o'er gleg at seeing fau'ts
In ithers, for ye ken
Perfection hasna yet been found
Amang the sons o' men.
The best o' us whiles gang ajee,
For human nature's frail,—
Then aye as far as ere you can
Let charity prevail.

The ninth commandment dinna break,
Nor dinna tell a lee—
A man's word should be just as guid
As what his oath should be.
The brightest ornament that gilds
The brow o' age or youth
Is that clear, shinin', sparklin' gem
That bears the name o' Truth;

Ne'er let your tongue to lewdness rin,
    Nor dinna be profane—
God winna haud you guiltless
    If ye tak' His name in vain.
If ye these maxims lay to heart
    You'll no gang far astray,
At least they'll be a help to you
    To guide you on your way.

Awa', Ye Warldly Crew.

Awa', ye warldly crew, wha think,
    As thro' the warld ye gang,
That if ye're only richt yoursel's
    There's naething can be wrang :
Ye base an' sordid, selfish loons,
    I plainly tell ye a',
If I could get my wull o' you,
    I'd gi'e your necks a thraw.

An' ye wha live by vice an' fraud,
    That disna care a preen
How muckle misery ye may cause
    If siller ye can glean :
Ne'er carin' how ye wrang the puir,
    Nor how ye break the law—
The muckle Deil wull get you yet,
    An' gi'e your necks a thraw.

Ye canting hypocrites wha tak'
    Religion for a cloak,
An' mak' the Kirk the means by which
    Ye cheat mair honest folk ;
Tak' ye my word, the time wull come
    You'll be despised by a',
An' few there are that care how soon
    Your necks may get a thraw.

An' you, ye loons, that in the Court
    Aft sweer that black is white,
An' try to mak' the wrang appear
    Mair virtuous than the right;
For purposes that suit yoursel's
    Ye twist an' turn the law—
Deil nor the Sheriff may get you
    To gi'e your necks a thraw.

An' ye wha canna keep your han's
    Frae out the public chest—
That gi'e the country a' the chaff
    While ye retain the grist—
Gi'e ow're your greedy, thievin' ways,
    An' do what's richt by a',
Or if ye dinna, feth I hope
    Your necks may get a thraw.

Eh, sure this warld is unco fu'
    O' knavery an' deceit;
I wonder when we'll learn to think
    " The guid alone are great;"
Let's hope the time o' which Burns sang
    May no far distant be,
When honest worth o'er a' the earth
    Shall always bear the gree.

The Lord Helps Them that Help Themsel's.

THE LORD helps them that help themsel's,
    And richt it is he should,
For them that winna help themsel's
    Will ne'er do muckle good.
The fiat has gone forth that ye
    Maun work to earn your bread,
And they that winna try to work
    Are lazy loons indeed.

There's some sits doon wi' faulded hands,
    Wi' neither bite nor sup,
Aye waitin' as Micawber did
    For "something to turn up."
They keep a' day within the house,
    Like snails within their shell,
And never think they've ony richt
    To try and help themsel'.

I canna see how they can sit,
    And live upon the hope
That manna will fa' doon frae heav'n
    To fill their am'ries up.
The days o' miracles are past,
    As maist o' folks can tell,
And they that winna work maun want,
    Sae rise and help yoursel'.

I'd ne'er refuse a worthy man
  A lift gaun up life's brae,
But charity is thrown awa'
  On a' sic sumphs as they ;
They should be taught that while they've health
  And strength, to use it well,
And ne'er depend on ither folks
  While they can help themsel'.

It's well enough, nae doubt, at times
  To trust to Providence ;
But they that lippen things like these
  Will show their want o' sense.
There's whiles ye may be out o' wark,
  Or hae a sickly spell,
In sic a case the Lord helps them
  That canna help themsel'.

The man o' independent mind
  Will try baith day and nicht
To help himsel' as far's he can
  In onything that's richt ;
Though lions roar upon his path,
  He disna mind their yell,
But bauldly pushes them aside
  And strives to help himsel'.

The bread you earn yoursel' is aye
  The sweetest to your taste—
Besides you are'na half sae apt
  To let aught gang to waste,

Then frien's and brithers ane‾and a',
Whaure'er ye chance to dwell,
Keep mind o' this, the Lord helps them
That try to help themsel'.

Be Honest Yoursel'.

BE HONEST, be honest, be trusty and true,
Though ithers gang gleyd that is naething to you ;
There are some ragged cowtes that will never do well ;
Ne'er be guided by them, but be honest yoursel'.

Be honest yoursel', and ne'er let greed o' gain
Mak' ye put oot your hand to tak' what's no your ain ;
If ye do, then to ruin you'll drive on pell-mell,
Whene'er you gae owre being honest yoursel'.

Riches got in this way never last very lang—
They come wi' the wind, wi' the water they gang,
And you canna expect that you'll e'er prosper well,
Unless you are upricht and honest yoursel'.

Be honest, though wealth never fa's to your share :
It's nae sin nor nae crime in a man to be puir ;
Though humble and lowly the cot where you dwell,
You'll meet wi' respect if you're honest yoursel'.

Be honest, and strive aye to do what is richt—
Ne'er do naething by day you can't stand by at nicht ;
Then your sleep will be pleasant and sound as a bell,
When you ken a' the time that you're honest yoursel'.

Be honest and faithfu', be truthfu' and wise—
The mean, petty doings o' tricksters despise ;
Keep your conscience as pure as a clear rinnin' well,
And aye aboon a' things be honest yoursel'.

Debt.

THERE is a mischief-makin' chiel
    That travels far and near,
And they wha ken him best ha'e learn'd
    To haud his name in fear.
If e'er he lays his claws on you,
    Awa' ye canna get :
You'll find it sae if ere ye meet
    Wi' that auld deevil, Debt.

His grip's as firm's a blacksmith's vice,
    And unco hard to break
He pu's ye doon as if he were
    A mill-stane roun' your neck.
He bangs ye richt and dings ye left,
    Till ye're sae sair beset
You dinna ken which way to turn
    To get awa' frae Debt.

He brings the duns unto your door,
    And whiles the bailiff, too,
Unwelcome visitors are they
    At ony time, I trow ;
They're greedy loons, for a' is fish
    That comes within their net,

They'll pick your banes as bare's your loof
Gin ye get into Debt.

A man may own a foolish wife,
    And yet some pleasure ha'e ;
He lives in hopes he'll see her gang
    Feet foremost owre the brae.
But hope deferr'd 'll mak' ye sick
    And gar ye foam and sweat,
If ance ye're in sae deep that ye
    Can ne'er get out o' Debt.

There's some it disna trouble much—
    They dinna seem to care
How much accumulates if they
    Can tak' on ony mair;
They're naethin' but a pack o' knaves
    That live upon their wit ;
An honest man will always try
    To pay an honest Debt.

I've liv'd within this planet now
    For thirty years and mair,
And aften to keep out o' debt
    I've struggled geyin' sair,
And though at ance I ne'er ha'e owned
    A hunder dollars yet,
I dinna care sae lang as I
    Can just keep out o' Debt.

O Fortune, ye're a glaikit jade,
    And blind as ony bat ;
You deal your favors roun' about,
    Ne'er kennin' what ye're at.
Gi'e rich folks less and puir folks mair
    Than they ha'e gotten yet,
And then we'll ha'e less cause to mourn
    O'er sic a thing as DEBT.

Do a' the Guid ye Can.

There's mony ups an' doons in life,
   Within this warld o' ours,
Our path is very aften strewed
   Wi' baith the thorns and flowers ;
Let's pick the roses frae the briers,
   Since life is but a span,
An' as ye gang alang the road,
   Do a' the guid ye can.

Misfortunes whiles 'll grip ye fast,
   An' snool ye gey'in sair ;
An' brawly do I ken mysel'
   They're unco hard to bear ;
But dinna let them fash ye much,
   You'll find whaure'er ye gang
There's some that's far waur aff than you—
   Do a' the guid ye can.

If fortune has been kind to you,
   Be thankfu' for its smiles,
An' dinna grudge to help alang
   The man that's dreed its wiles.
If honest poverty you meet,
   Haud out a helpin' han' ;
You only do what's richt when ye
   Do a' the guid ye can.

There's some you'll meet wi' now an' then
    Sunk in the mire o' sin ;
It is your privilege to try
    An' draw them out again ;
Tho' they may mak' sair slips at times,
    Ne'er shun your fellow-man,
Christ died for them as weel as you—
    Do a' the guid ye can.

If there's a blessin' fa's on earth,
    'Tis that which mercy earns ;
Then dinna e'er forget that we
    " Are a' John Tamson's bairns."*
This warld would be a happy place,
    Just like a fairy lan',
If ilka ane would try an' aye
    Do a' the guid they can.

'Twas said lang syne by Ane that ken't,
    An' what He says believe,
'Tis better far at ony time
    To gi'e than to receive.
Then O be sure ye bear in min'
    To follow mercy's plan,
An' to the utmost o' your power
    Do a' the guid ye can.

---

* An expression equivalent to saying we are all of the same family.

The Wheel within a Wheel.

There's aye a wheel within a wheel
  Whichever way we turn,
And they wha ken the way it works
  Ha'e little cause to mourn.
To find out a' the secrets o't
  Would tak' a clever chiel ;
There's just a special few can work
  The wheel within a wheel.

The wily politician tries
  To mak' it understood
He serves his country a' his micht
  For just his country's good ;
I notice, when he gets a chance,
  He serves himsel' wi' zeal—
He kens the way to turn aroun'
  The wheel within a wheel.

I winna say they're a' alike,
  But ae thing weel I ken
Self-interest predominates
  Amang maist kinds o' men ;
Nae doot you'll meet wi' now and then
  An' honest, worthy chiel

Wha scorns to tak' advantage o'
The wheel within a wheel.

The man o' business, when he strives
    To get his fortune made,
Is ne'er content till by some means
    He corners you in trade ;
He mak's a " ring " wi' twa-three frien's
    Wha understan' it weel,
Then at a given signal turns
    The wheel within a wheel.

There's mony mair that I could name,
    And a' their daily care
Is how to work the oracle
    And mak' their muckle mair ;
It never ance comes in their heids
    To think o' ithers' weal—
They sit a' day and screw and turn
    The wheel within a wheel.

And e'en some clergymen themsel's
    Will prove you frae the Word—
When siller's in the case—how they've
    Been " called " on by the Lord ;
But, God forgi'e me, whiles I think
    The " call " comes frae the deil—
He's aye the ane that puts in gear
    The wheel within a wheel.

Say what you like, gang whaur you will,
   God Mammon reigns supreme,
And he's maist thocht o' wha can soom
   The best doon Fortune's stream.
Oh ! but I weary for the time
   When man to man shall feel
As brithers should, and throw awa'
   The wheel within a wheel !

I'm a Glasco Chappie.

(On being asked what part of Scotland I came from.)

I'm a Glasco chap (I'll ne'er deny it),
    I'll fecht ye till I dee,
Sae I would hae ye a' to ken
    That ye maunna meddle me.
I winna fecht for fechtin's sake,
    But if I ance begin,
I'll stan' my grun' as lang's I can,
    And try my best to win.

I like to fecht the battles o'
    The weak against the strong,
Although I'll ne'er tak' sides wi' them
    I think are in the wrong ;
But show me that your cause is richt,
    And say "mak' this your plea,"
Wi' a' my heart an' a' my saul
    I'll fecht for't till I dee.

This life is but a fecht at best,
    For six days out o' seven
We hae to warsel a' the time
    To try an' mak' a lievin ;
Some win their way to wealth and fame
    That don't deserve't ava,

While honest merit gey an' aft
  Is chirted to the wa'.

Though Glasco folk are fechtin' folk,
  They're kind an' honest, too :
They've ae wee faut—they like their maut,
  An' sometimes they get fou ;
But deil-ma-care, you'll find them men
  On whom you can rely,
Although an odd ane here an' there
  Is not the "real Mackay."

It's now some three-and-twenty years
  Since last I saw the Clyde,
But aft since then my heart has yearn'd
  To wander by its side.
It may be that I'll see't nae mair,
  But come or gang what will,
My earnest, heartfelt wish shall be—
  " LET GLASGOW FLOURISH" still,

A Mither's Troubles.

Whaur ha'e ye been the lee-lang day,
    Ye little ne'er-do-weel ?
I ha'e a min' to skelp ye sair
    Until I gar ye squeal ;
Ae sicht o' you I ha'ena seen
    Sin' breakfast time this morn ;
I think that sic a steerin' wean
    As you has ne'er been born.

Whaur ha'e ye been, ye mischief, that
    Ye've got in sic a plight ?
If I wud tak' the tause to you
    It just wud ser' ye right.
The claes that ye got on this morn,
    That look'd sae clean an' braw,
Are cover'd o'er wi' dirt an' glaur—
    Yer jacket's torn in twa !

"Ye couldna help it ?"   Haud yer tongue
    An' tell me nae sic lee ;
You look just like as if ye had
    Been sclimbin' up a tree.
An' there's yer shoon, no three weeks auld,
    That's oot at baith the taes ;

'Twould tak' a fortune, I declare,
   To keep ye gaun in claes.

" Ye're awfu' hungry?"   Like enough ;
   Why did ye no come hame ?
It shows you think mair o' yer play
   Than ye do o' yer wame.
" Ye want a daud o' tattie scone?"
   My certe ye're no blate ;
I wish the schule was in again,
   To keep ye aff the street.

Losh ! here is something else.   What next !
   Ye've riven a' your breeks ;
God help the woman that has weans
   That ony comfort seeks !
For she may fecht, an' toil, an' work
   Her fingers to the bane—
Then gang to bed, an' rise next day,
   An' just begin again.

Come till I tosh ye up again,
   An' kame your touzie hair,
" That hurts ye?"   Haud yer tongue, or feth
   I'll maybe hurt ye mair.
What will yer faither say, think ye,
   When he comes hame at e'en,
An' I ha'e tauld him a ye've dune,
   An' a' whaur ye ha'e been ?

What's that ye say ?   " Don't tell him, an
  " Ye'll be as guid's ye can,
" An' that ye'll aye do richt by me
  " When ye grow up a man ?"
Weel, weel, ye'll maybe gather sense
  When ye're a wee thocht bigger.
Noo, rin to Peter Patterson's,
  An' bring twa pund o' sugar.

A Cheerie Engle-side.

Gi'e Fame and Fortune unto them
　　Wha glory in their name ;
I sing a joy aboon them baith
　　That can be found at hame :
A joy in which an honest man
　　Can tak' an honest pride—
A loving wife, and loving weans,
　　And cheerie ingle-side.

Ambition's charms may lure ye on,
　　And please ye for a while,
But a' that glitters isna gowd—
　　They're aften fu' o' guile ;
Throw them awa' if ye prefer
　　Thro' life to smoothly glide—
You'll find mair heart-felt pleasure in
　　A cheerie ingle-side.

Wealth winna bring you peace o' mind,
　　Nor ease a heart that's sair,
And Fame is but an empty sound
　　That melts awa' in air ;
But whaur the sacred lowe o' love
　　Burns bricht at even-tide,
It casts a gleam o' joy and mak's
　　A cheerie ingle-side.

It's no the tinsel'd works o' art
    That hang around your wa',
Nor Brussels spread upon your floor,
    Bring happiness ava ;
You may ha'e gear o' every kind
    That siller can provide,
And ne'er ken what it means to ha'e
    A cheerie ingle-side.

A' ye that's got a cantie wife,
    And cosie " but " and " ben,"
Wi' twa-three " totums " rinning round,
    As weel as me, ye ken,—
It's loving looks and winning smiles,
    And tongues that winna chide,
That bring content and mak' the bliss
    Around the ingle-side.

Then whether ye're in quest o' wealth,
    Or gang in search o' fame,
Ne'er let them cause ye to neglect
    The pleasures o' your hame ;
For, tak' my word, ye winna find,
    Tho' ye gang far and wide,
A joy mair blest than can be found
    Around the ingle-side.

O Fortune ! I ha'e ne'er, as yet,
    Cam' begging to your door,
Nor do I ken what ye for me
    May ha'e laid up in store ;

But now I'm gaun to ask that you
  Extend your favors wide—
Gi'e ilka honest man and wife
  A cheerie ingle-side.

Crape on the Door.

There's a little white cottage that stan's 'mang the trees,
Whaur the humming-bird comes to sip sweets wi' the bees,
Whaur the bright morning-glories grow up o'er the eaves,
And the wee birdies nestle amang the green leaves.
But there's something around it to-day that seems sad—
It hasna that look o' contentment it had ;
There is gloom whaur there used to be sunshine before ;
Its windows are darkened—there's crape on the door.

There is crape on the door—all is silent within ;
There are nae merry children there makin' a din ;
For the ane that was merriest aye o' them a'
Is laid out in robes that look white as the sna'.
But yesterday morn, when the sun shone sae bright,
Nae step bounded freer—nae heart was mair light ;
When the gloamin' cam' round, a' his playing was o'er—
He was drowned in the burn—sae there's crape on the door.

Nae mair will he skip like a lamb o'er the lea,
Or pu' the wild flowers, or gang chasin' the bee ;
He'll be miss'd by the bairns when they come hame frae schule,
For he met them ilk day coming doon o'er the hill.
Beside his wee coffin his lone mother kneels,
And she breathes forth a prayer for the sorrow she feels ;
Her puir widowed heart has been seared to the core,
For not lang sinsyne there was crape on the door.

Her sobs choke her utt'rance, though she strives, but in vain,
To stifle her grief, or her tears to restrain ;
Yet she lovingly murmurs, " I winna repine;
Thy will be done, Father; Thy will and not mine ;
Though my trials are great, yet I winna complain,
For I ken that the Lord has but ta'en back his ain,
To dwell wi' the angels above evermore,
Whaur there's nae sin nor sorrow, nor crape on the door."

As ye Sow, so shall ye Reap.

This life's made up o' guid and bad,
  But mony are the ills
Which by our want of wisdom that
  We bring upon oursel's ;
We aft lose sight of what we should
  Within our memory keep—
That is, whatever we may sow
  That also shall we reap.

Ye that are in your Spring, tak care
  What seeds you cast abroad,
That when your Autumn time comes roun'
  Your harvest may be good ;
And aye tak' heed nae fulsome weeds
  Amang your seedlings creep,
For whatsoever ye may sow
  That also shall ye reap.

See that ye dinna sow the seeds
  O' discord and o' strife,
But plant " good will to men," that ye
  May comfort ha'e through life.
The ane will bring ye peace and joy,
  The ither gar ye weep,
For surely if ye sow the wind,
  The whirlwind ye maun reap.

Ye canna cheat the Lord wi' what
　　Ye in the ground may fling—
Figs winna grow on thistles, nor
　　Will grapes frae brambles spring ;
For ilka seed is watched by Him,
　　He never is asleep,
And rest assur'd whate'er ye sow
　　That also shall ye reap.

It may seem up-hill work at first,
　　But dinna think it hard,
For virtue at the last is sure
　　To bring its ain reward ;
Then pick the seed that's fresh and pure,
　　And plough your furrows deep,
And bear in mind whate'er ye sow
　　That also shall ye reap.

Wee Tot.

OUR wee Tot took sick, an' she wasted awa,
An' we couldna tell what had come o'er her ava ;
Her bonnie blue e'e that aye sparkled sae clear
Grew dim, an' her mither's was wat wi' a tear,
As she sat thro' the lang nicht an' watched by her cot,
An' my ain wasna dry when I look'd on wee Tot.

Wee Tot was the life o' our cheerie fire-en'
As she toddled about thro' our " but" an' our " ben ;"
She was playfu' an' pawkie, auldfarrant an' slee,
An' the joy an' the pride o' her mither an' me ;
An' we felt mair contented an' pleased wi' our lot
Frae the time heaven sent us our bonnie wee Tot.

When the bloom left her cheek we were waefu' an' sad,—
To bring't back we would gi'en a' the siller we had.
I miss'd her saft kiss when I cam' hame at e'en,
Tired an' weary sometimes, when my days' wark was dune ;
An' my wee drap o' tea, aye, seemed cauld tho' 'twere hot,—
An' tasteless, an' fusionless, wantin' wee Tot.

The doctor was sent for an' quickly he cam'—
(The half o' thae doctors are nought but a sham)—
He hum'd an' he haw'd, just as much as to say
" There's no muckle left for ye now but to pray ;
I doot that ye'll hae to put up wi' yer lot,
An' mak' up your min's for to part wi' wee Tot."

Her grannie cam' in frae the country next day ;
(She'd been in lang before—but she lived far away,)
She brought twa-three " simples" row'd up in her pouch,
That acted like magic amaist at her touch.
E'er twa days had passed by, wi' the care that she got,
We could see quite a change in our bonnie wee Tot.

This raised up our hopes, an' we still did our best,
An' trusted to God He would do a' the rest ;
An' He (in his mercy), relieved a' our cares,—
He was gracious an' kind, for He answered our prayers ;
An', wi' auld grannie's help, our sweet winsome wee wean
Is as hale now an' hearty as ever again.

My blessin' on women folk o'er a' the earth ;
In the time o' our need we find out what they're worth ;
Then the form o' a min'st'ring angel they take.
I'll aye loe the auld anes for auld grannie's sake—
For the young anes, I wish joy may fa' to their lot,
An' a couthie gudeman an' a bloomin' wee Tot.

Grandpa's Pet.

"WEE, curly-headed, tottin' thing,
  That's aye sae tosh an' neat an' clean,
Sae fu' o' mischief an' o' fun—
  Joy's dancin' in your very een.
To sit an' watch thy pawkie tricks
  Aft fills my ain heart fu' o' joy,
An' gars me think o' days gane by,
  When mirth was free frae care's alloy.

"Frae morn to e'en ye're rinnin' roun'
  As brisk an' happy as a bee;
Unless whiles when ye crack your croon,
  There's ne'er a tear-drap dims your 'ee.
Ye're licht o' foot, an' licht o' heart—
  Aye in a merry, happy vein;
Fun seems to to be your chief employ,
  Hech! sirs, but ye're an unco wean.

"Be still, you wee, mischievous rogue;
  What's that ye're knockin' on the wa'?
Deil's in the callan! sure as death
  He's broke my cutty pipe in twa.
Ay, ye may rin. Tak' care, tak' care:
  See what ye've dune—ye've tumble't o'er
The three-legged stool. That's twice the day
  Ye've skailt my snuff upon the floor."

"Ye're sorry noo?" "Sae should you be;
 Come here an' sit upon my knee :
I wonner whiles ye ar'na tired—
 Sit doon an' tak' a rest awee.
Let go my specs—ye'll break them too—
 An' keep your han's out o' my hair;
Your nails, I fin', are geyin' sharp,
  When they gang in a part that's bare.

"Sit doon, an' be at peace awhile,
 I want to read a verse or twa.
Na heth, ye canna be at rest
  There is nae stoppin' ye ava.
There's naethin' sacred unto you
  That ye can lay your han's upon.
Ye search the Scriptures, that's a fact—
  If I read Matthew ye want John.

"Lay doon the book ! weel, weel, what next?"
 "Please, Gran'pa, to tak' aff my shoon,"
"Wha' tied them up in sic a knot?"
  " Ye dinna ken how it was dune?"
" It's like a Gordian knot to me,
 I canna get it loused ava ;
Ye'll hae to gang an' bring the shears,
  Until I cut the lace in twa.

"There, that's a' richt." Sing 'hush-a-bye.'
 " O, Gran'pa ! I forgot my prayers.
This night I lay me down to sleep "—
  (That's pussy comin' doon the stairs.)

" Wheesht ! shut your een "—" My soul to keep ;
 If I should die before I wake "—
(I never kiss'd my pa or ma)—
 " Take me to heaven for Jesus' sake."

"There, that'll do.   Noo rin awa'
 An' kiss them, an' come back again,
An' gang to sleep upon my knee."
 "Ye did it?"   "That's a clever wean !
Come, cuddle in my bosie, noo ;
 Your troubles for the day are past ;
Puir, silly thing, ye're unco tired,
 An' lyin' soun' asleep at last !

" I look into your face an' see
 The image o' ane deid an' gane ;
I was as proud o' him as thee,
 When first he toddled a' his lane ;
But years hae passed since I hae smoothed
 The curls that graced his bonnie broo,
An' she, wha would hae lo'ed ye baith,
 Is up in heaven wi' him noo.

" I wonner whiles, my bonnie bairn,
 If ye'll to guid or ill incline,
Or how much sorrow ye may dree
 Ere your hair is as white as mine.
I ken I'm turning auld an' frail—
 My days are drawin' to an en' ;
I've seen the allotted time o' man—
 My years are noo threescore an' ten.

"I haena much to leave you, bairn,
  But ye've nae heritage o' shame ;
Altho' I say it o' mysel',
  I've borne aye an honest name.
May virtue guide your steps ! and, oh !
  May Heaven its blessin's on you shed !
Till ye have seen your bairns' bairns.
  (Here, Leezie, lay the wean in bed.)"

The Real Sandy Mackay.

Preachin' and practice are twa different things,
    And they're aften placed widely apart ;
I canna help noticing whiles that what springs
    Frae the tongue has nae root in the heart.
It's easy enough aye to gie guid advice,
    Maist o' folks can do that when they try :
           But faith without wark
           Shows ye're still in the dark,
For it's no' the real Sandy Mackay. *

The Deil tak' a' them that gang slinkin' aroun'
    Wi' a sweet pleasant smile on their face,
Aye tryin' at a' times to rin ithers doon,
    While they keep themsel's oot o' disgrace ;
That man is a rogue and a knave in his heart
    That slanders his freen's on the sly.
           Never speak to him mair,
           He's not worthy your care,
For he's no' the real Sandy Mackay.

A grocer may put a few pounds in his pouch
    By gi'ein' licht wecht now and then ;
He may ne'er be found oot till he maks himself rich
    But it's no' dealing justly by men.

---

* An expression used in some parts of Scotland, equal to saying " it is not the real thing."

If there's ony in toon (and it may be there's some)
  To whom these last lines would apply,
      Let them alter their ways
      A' the rest o' their days,
For it's no' the real Sandy Mackay.

A merchant that maks his ten thousan' a year,
  And yet thinks that he canna pay
The men that work for him, perhaps ony mair
  Than just four or five shillin's a day,
If he lives a' the time on the fat o' the land,
  While they gang baith hungry and dry,
      You may say what you will,
      But, I stick to it still,
He's no' the real Sandy Mackay.

No, Sandy Mackay is a douce decent man,
  And there's naethin' about him that's mean ;
He's kind and warm-hearted and hauds oot his han'
  When he sees you're in want o' a freen'.
If you meet wi' a man that is honest and fair,
  Ane that does as he would be done by,
      Wear him next to your heart,
      Wi' his love never part,
For he's the real Sandy Mackay.

The Nearer the Kirk the Farther from Grace.

THERE'S a saying that's nearly as auld as the hills,
    But it stan's just as true to this day,
And that is the nearer you live to the kirk
    The farther frae grace you're away.
You'll often see them that's been raised 'neath its wings
    Turning oot what we ca' a hard case ;
Tho' their heids may be crammed wi' the learning o' books
    Yet their hearts are devoid of a' grace.

There's plenty that try aye to mak' you believe
    That they're leading the life o' a saint,
When they're naething but wolves blaain' oot like a sheep,
    And they never wax weary or faint.
Tho' they gang to the kirk ilka day in the year,
    Yet that disna alter the case ;
You may sit on the tap of the steeple and sing,
    And still be a lang way frae grace.

Sic people may preach until doomsday comes roun',
    But gin they dinna practice as weel,
It shows that they dinna believe what they say,
    And they're gaun just as straught to the decl.
Its of nae use ava to gang whining aroun'
    Wi' a lang sanctimonious face ;
You may baith preach and pray every hour in the day
    And yet be a lang way frae grace.

And gin ye should speer how to draw nearer grace,
   I will tell ye a plain simple way :
Do justly, walk humbly, show mercy to a',
   Tho' they whiles gang a " wee thocht" astray.
It is human to err, but 'tis God-like, ye ken,
   To forgie ; then let such be your case :
When you worship the Lord wi' your deeds, not your words,
   Then you're drawing mair near to His grace.

An Epistle.

(To D. Manwell, York Mills, State of New York.)

DEAR SIR :

WARK for the nicht I've laid aside,
An' my Pegasus got astride ;
It's noo sae lang since last I rode him,
The Deil himsel could scarcely haud him ;
He jumps about frae left to right—
You'd think the beast had gane clean gyte ;
In sober pace I fain would trot him,
But for my saul I canna get him
To jog alang, or even canter,
But aff he gangs like Tam O'Shanter's
Auld Mare Meg, when she was rinnin'
An' Cutty Sark behind her grinnin',
An' Tam, puir chiel, was sittin' sweatin'
Wi' *dread o' that black imp o' Satan.*
My warst wish on the wrinkled hag,
For pu'in the tail frae sic a nag ;
For e'en though Maggie had had mair o't,
'Twas worth a guinea every hair o't ;
But na doot Cutty Sark had use for't,
Or she would ne'er run sic a race for't—
Perhaps she wanted Maggie's tail
To mak' a soap brush for the Deil,

Or kept it for to fan hersel',
(If sic a thing is used in h—l)
Whilk's no unlikely, for I hear,
It's unco het at times down there.

But noo Pegasus' pace is mended,
His harum scarum race is ended;
And while he gently trots alang,
I'll e'en begin and sing my sang.
I've heard, Sir, that ye hae been lying',
Nae, mair, that ye've been nearly dyin',
An' that grim carlin ca'd auld Nickie
Was thinkin', nae doot, very quick he
Would hae ye safe within his clutches,
To whistle jigs to ghaists an' witches;
But by my troth, my brimstone freen'
He's thrawn the glamour o'er your e'en,
For Manwell's up an' hale an' weel,
An' fears nae neither man nor deil;
At ony rate, ye ill-faur'd crew,
Dee when he likes he's no for you.

" Ye powers that mak' mankind your care,"
Wi' Manwell a' your blessings share;
Tak' tent o' him, for he's a man
That's been formed after " Nature's plan;"
An' chiels like him are seldom seen,
At least they're few and far between;
Lang let him live, an' when he dees
Up 'mang yoursel's gie him a heese;

For them doon-by he canna bide them,
An' dis'na want to be beside them.
Nae mair do I your humble servan',
Though o' your favors less deservin',
But if ye've room an' ye can spare it,
Wi' Davie I would like to share it ;
For fain am I to be beside him,
Through weal or woe whate'er betide him.

Next on the list noo comes your wife,
The joy and comfort of your life ;
An', Manwell, dinna think I flatter,
Ye may be guid but she is better ;
She's nane o' them, Sir, that gangs roun'
Baith day and nicht frae toon to toon,
Displaying a' their whigmaleeries,
To gar men's heads spin roun' like peeries ;
An' shawin' aff their eloquence,
An' a' they hae but common sense ;
Raisin' conventions, makin' speeches,
Claiming their richt to wear the breeches—
Their richts be hanged ! 'twould serve them weel
To shake them a' within a creel ;
Or may be what would suit them better,
To dook them in a pail o' water,
An' set the bairns to jeer and daff them,
Till ance't they got the clockin aff them.

O would they tak' yours for a sample,
She'd set them a' a guid example ;

Instead o' gaun roun' makin' speeches,
Dressed up in bloomer hats and breeches,
Dining wi' editors an' pastors,
Crammin' their wames wi' clams an' oysters,
She'd teach them how to mend a sark,
An' ither kinds o' household wark;
Whilk's mair becomin' o' their station,
Than makin' laws to rule a nation.

But if they want to try their han'
At makin' laws, I'm no the man
To say them nay; Indeed I'd rather
They'd send the hale pack aff thegither,
An' at their head put Lucy Stone,
That bold, undaunted Amazon;
Unto Newfoundland tak' the road,
To settle this question 'bout the cod;
Or aff across the Atlantic main,
To try an' pick a King for Spain—
It may be that wi' a' their clatters
They'd beat the men at sic like matters.

But, Sir, I'll hae to quat my sang,
For fear I may say aught that's wrang;
Meanwhile, I wish you hale and weel—
Lang may you live, my canty chiel;
May peace an' comfort still be yours,
Content be aye within your doors—
May poverty ne'er learn the road,
That tak's him doon to your abode;

An' after mony years hae past,
An' ye are ta'en awa at last,
An' lyin' number'd wi' the deid,
We'll raise a stane aboon your heid,
Whaur ilka ane may proudly scan—
" HERE LIES A WORTHY, HONEST MAN."

To Wm. Murray, Esq., Hamilton.

AUTHOR OF A POEM ENTITLED THE "SCOTTISH PLAID."

DEAR SIR, I've read your plaidie thro',
And think a guid deal o' it, too.
It is the best I've seen frae you
         This year or mair.
If credit's gi'en whaur credit's due,
         Ye'll get your share.

Ye ken I'm no inclined to flatter;
I'd rather live on bread and water,
Than wi' fause praise a man bespatter
         To gain a fee,
Or try to mak' my tongue to utter
         A fulsome lee.

Sae ye'll believe me when I say
I like your hamely cantie lay.
It minds me o' a bygane day,
         When I took pride
To wander out at gloamin' gray,
         Wrapp'd in my plaid.

But Scottish bards will never lose
Their love for plaids or Athol brose;
I'd take the rascal by the nose
         That would deride

Whate're such bards as you compose
     Aboot the plaid.

Ye've read, when Burns was young and crouse,
That Mrs. Scott, o' Wauchope Hoose,
Presented him, for his ain use,
     A gaucy plaid :
Wi't on him, aft he woo'd the Muse
     By Lugar's side.

O, Burns ! thou bard aboon a' ithers,
That wanted mankind to be brithers,
A' ae man's bairns, tho' different mithers ;
     Lang will ye shine.
The rhymes we mak' are only blethers
     Compared wi' thine.

There's mony mair that I could name,
That claimed auld Scotia for their hame—
Men wha had trod the path of fame
     Before they died—
Wha thocht it honor, not a shame,
     To wear a plaid.

Bear witness, Campbell, Motherwell,
And thou, sweet-songster Tannahill ;
Scott, Hogg and Ramsay, and Macneil,
     Men truly great.
Nae bards that climb'd Parnassus' hill,
     Ere sang mair sweet.

But we can ne'er expect to shine
In sic a worthy, honor'd line
O' bards like these ; but never min',
      We'll do our best,
And court the favors o' the Nine
      Amang the rest.

But, sir, ye'll think I'm daft, I fear.
Lang may you hae a plaid to wear,
And may you aye, frae year to year,
      Add to your fame,
Until a' worthy folk revere
      " My Murray's " name.

To Adam Brown, Esq., Hamilton, on his Return from Scotland.

RESPECTED SIR—

        I've heard you've been
  Across the saut sea faem,
To spend the summer months 'mang scenes
  And freens you lo'ed *at hame*.
I'm glad you hae got back again,
  And welcom'd will you be
By a' your freen's in Canada—
  And nane mair sae than me.

Stan's Scotland whaur she did, my freen',
  Or is her glory fled?
Does auld Ben Nevis, 'mang the clouds,
  Still raise his rev'rent head ?
Does a' her tow'ring heath-clad hills
  Still stan' erect and free—
Her cascades, streams, and mountain rills .
  Still rin to join the sea?

Stan's Scotland whaur she did, my freen'?
  Come tell me, gin you ken,
If aye the same auld spirit reigns
  On mountain, moor and glen?
Does "Scots wha hae wi' Wallace bled"
  Still cheer her on her road ;

Has she still men wha daur to tread
    The path which Knox has trod ?

Stan's Scotland whaur she did, my freen',
    As in the days lang syne,
When her brave sons—proud, fearless ones—
    Hae shed their bluid like wine ?
Does she still battle for the " richt,"
    Opposing a' that's wrang ?
Does " Corra Linn,"* wi' merry din
    Aye sing the same auld sang ?

Stan's Scotland whaur she did, my freen' ?
    Oh ! how I'd like to see
The place whaur " Castle Dangerous,"† stan's ;
    It's unco dear to me.
Oh ! for ae balmy day in June,
    When nature's in its pride,
Just ae lang summer afternoon
    To wander by the Clyde.

I'd like to see the " Brigs o' Ayr,"
    And that auld haunted Kirk
Whaur Tam O'Shanter stood and glowr'd
    At witches thro' the mirk ;
I'd like to see the "thackit cot,"
    To which the whole world turns,
And kneel beside that sacred spot
    Whaur lies our Minstrel Burns.

* The Falls of Clyde.
† The Castle of the Douglass'.

I'd like to stan' on " Ettrick's Banks,"
  Or whaur the " Yarrow " flows;
Or on the field of Bannockburn
  Whaur Scotland drubb'd her foes ;
And I could spend a day or twa,
  Or may be even three,
Whaur Claverhouse, that daring Deil,
  Gaed riding thro' Dundee.

I'd like to speel Ben Lomond's side,
  Whaur bold Macgregors dwell,
Or spend a canny hour within
  Dumbarton's bonnie dell.
Auld Stirling's towers, Dunedin's bowers—
  I'd like to see them a',
And hear the surges as they roar
  And sweep o'er Berwick-Law.

It's five-and-twenty year since I
  Auld Scotia's hills hae trod ;
I sometimes doubt I ne'er will see
  The daisy deck her sod ;
But if Dame Fortune kind should prove
  And health be spared to me,
I'll hear her linties sing again
  Ance mair before I dee.

To Mr. Paul Stuart, Wood Market.

My worthy, kind, obliging friend,
I wish that you would try and send
Me down anither load o' wood,
And o' be sure you send it good;
But if you dinna, Lord forgie ye,
For I will show nae mercy to ye.

In times like these, when siller's scarce,
And credit's just as bad, or worse,
A man requires to think sometimes
Before he parts wi' a' his dimes,
For deil tak' me if ever I
Can get a dollar to lay by,

Or else I'd mak' ye send me doon
Enough to last the hale year roun'.
But just at present I maun say
One cord will be enough to-day;
Some ither time, when siller's plenty,
I'll maybe mak' you send me twenty.

I had amaist forgot to say
I dinna want it right away;
I hae as much as put me thro'
At least anither week or two;
But if you see a chance that's fair,
And you hae got the time to spare,

Then send it doon without delay,
I'm ready for it ony day;
Be sure you send me number one,
And get it just as cheap's you can.

And now good-bye, my friend and brither,
When next we meet wi' ane anither,
We'll maybe hae a drap thegither.
Meantime I am with love most fervent,
Your most obliged and humble servant.

My Mither's Advice.

MY MITHER ! God bless her ! (she's deid noo and gane),
    Was counted baith worthy and wise ;
When fechting the battle o' life at her side,
    She aften gied me her advice ;
And, amang ither things, she would say to me whiles,
    Noo, laddie, keep mind o' this well,
Be sure o' the pennies you aye tak' good care,
    And the pounds 'll tak' care o' themsel'.

Sma' beginnings at first mak' big endings at last,
    If you use ony gumption or care,
And you'll like it gey weel when a "rainy day" comes,
    If you've twa-three bawbees you can to spare.
It's a puir way to live—frae your hand to your mouth,—
    You will find that it ne'er answers well,
Sae be sure o' the pennies you aye tak' good care,
    And the pounds 'll tak' care o' themsel'.

It's best to be carefu' and thrifty and wise,
    And live aye inside o' your means ;
The shorter you keep your accounts by the heid
    You'll be thocht the mair o' by your frien's ;
Gin you get in their debt then it winna be lang
    Ere they screed aff your fauts by the ell,
Sae be sure o' the pennies you aye tak' guid care,
    And the pounds 'll tak' care o' themsel'.

Ne'er be greedy, nor graspin', nor e'er do what's wrang
    To get siller to put in your pouch ;
I don't want you to think that the chief end o' man
    Is merely to lee and get rich ;
But be steady, industrious, and work hard and save,
    Sae that comfort may be whaur you dwell,
And be sure o' the pennies you aye tak' guid care,
    And the pounds 'll tak' care o' themsel',

Be sure and be honest, and strive aye to be
    Independent as far as you can ;
Try and mak' your ain way through the world, and then
    You can haud up your heid like a man.
But ne'er turn your back on a worthy auld frien',
    Though he may need your help for a spell—
Its better if you can gie ithers your help,
    Than be needing that help for yoursel'.

I've kept mind o' her words, but truth mak's me say
    That I ne'er could accumulate gear,
Let me do as I would I was aye just as puir
    At the end o' ilk following year ;
It may be that I've been a guid deal to blame,
    For not looking after it well,
But the pennies were aye geyin' scarce, and somehow
    The pounds kept awa' by themsel'.

But I'd say to a' them that are starting in life,
    (Though it ne'er has done me muckle guid),
To tak' care o' the bawbees that pass through your hands,
    For you never ken what you may need ;

The best o' us meet with mishanters at times,
  Which the wisest folk canna foretel,
Then be sure o' the pennies you aye tak' guid care,
  And the pounds 'll tak' care o' themsel'.

There's Mickle Cry and Little Woo.

THERE'S mickle cry and there's little woo,
The auld wife said when she clipp'd her sow,
And it's just the same the hale world through,
There's aye mair cry than what there's woo.

It's true, although it strange may seem,
That "bunkum" always reigns supreme ;
O' specimens I'll gie a few,
Wherein there's aye mair cry than woo.

The politician waxes warm,
When he rides his hobby o' reform,
And he tells you a' that he's gaun to do,
But there's mickle cry and there's little woo.

Revivalists strange pliskies play,
To catch the sheep that's gaun astray ;
They may do guid unto a few,
But there's aye mair cry than there is woo.

Philanthropists hae aye some scheme
The world and mankind to redeem ;
But gin you sift their actions thro',
There's aften far mair cry than woo.

Our missionaries preach and pray,
And tell us always that they hae
"Great expectations" frae Ya-hoo,
But still there's aye mair cry than woo.

Their schemes are guid enough nae doot,
If they were fairly carried oot,
But when you look at what they do,
You'll find there's aye mair cry than woo.

Our statesmen always promise fair
O' "guid times coming" every year ;
Their promises they aye fa' thro',
There's mickle cry and there's little woo.

Our Gladstanes, Brights and Disraelis,
Nae doot but what they're clever fellows ;
They may mean weel in a' they do,
But still there's aye mair cry than woo.

The Press pretends to lead the way
On a' the questions of the day
That has the "public weal" in view,
But feth there's aye mair cry than woo.

And sae it is the wide world o'er,
Men fecht and talk and mak' a splore,
And ane anither's lugs they pu',
And mak' great cry 'bout little woo.

I ha'ena mickle sense mysel',
But yet I ken, and ken fu' well,
The auld wife's sayin' still hauds true,
There's aye mair cry than what there's woo.

If ilka ane would tak' in han'
To do whatever guid they can,
And honest be in a' they do,
We'd ha'e less cry and far mair woo.

O Canada, I wish you weel—
To you my heart is true and leal;
May a' your sons and daughters too
Ha'e little cry and mickle woo.

Tak' Things as They Come.

Contentment is a happy thing,
    And they wha hae't are blest ;
It mak's nae odds how things may gang,
    Their minds are aye at rest,—
Be 't guid or bad it's a' the same,
    They never fash their thoom,
But jouk their heads and let it pass,
    And tak things as they come.

Sufficient for ilk day is aye
    The ill it brings alang ;
Then dinna ye mak' o' your griefs
    A never-ending sang.
Draw in your stool beside the fire,
    Let care gae up the lum,
Sit doon and smoke your pipe in peace,
    And tak' things as they come.

Ye maunna think that you'll get leave
    To lie in Fortune's lap,
An' bask forever in her smiles
    An' ne'er meet wi' mishap.
The willfu' jade is fu' o' tricks,
    An' while's she'll play you some
That's hard to bear, sae ye maun learn
    To tak' things as they come.

I dinna want ye to sit doon
    An' feed yoursel's on hope,
Nor idly waste awa' your time,
    But gi'e your talents scope—
Put oot your han' an' help yoursel',
    Don't stan' as ye were num',
First do what's richt, then be content,
    An' tak' things as they come.

Dinna Despair.

KEEP up your heart, keep up your heart,
    An' dinna be downcast,
Tho' ablins ye hae care's enow'—
    They winna always last;
An' dinna ye gi'e way to grief,
    Whatever may betide,—
Tho' dark's the nicht the mornin's licht,
    There's aye a sunny side.

The loss o' wife, the loss o' weans,
    The loss o' gowd an' gear,
An' ither things that ye may dree,
    May try ye gey severe;
Afflictions are the means by which
    Our faith is purified;
Tho' dark an' dowie whiles they seem,
    There's aye a sunny side.

Curse God and die, Job's tempters said,
    When he was sair oppress't,
An' mickle grief had he to bear
    Ere they could shake his trust;
He kenn'd fu' weel the end would come
    On which he had relied,
While peerin' thro' the murky gloom
    He saw the sunny side.

There is a Providence aboon
    That watches o'er us a',
That winna let unto the grun'
    A wee bit sparrow fa'
Without He kens ; an' disna' He
    For a' our wants provide ?
An' tho' His face is hid at times,
    There's aye a sunny side.

Then leave your troubles a' to Him
    An' set your min's at rest,
Believin' aye that a' that's sent
    Will turn out for the best ;
Let virtue be your guidin' star
    As doon life's stream ye glide,
An' dinna doubt but at the end
    Ye'll find the sunny side.

Our Wee Jeanie.

THE tears come pappin' o'er my cheeks,
    Sometimes when I'm alane,
Whene'er I think on our bonnie bairn,
    That awa' frae us was ta'en.
She's lying now in the cauld kirkyard,
    Wi' the grass aboon her heid ;
And mony a waefu' thocht I've had
    Since our wee bairnie dee'd.

She was na lang in this warld with us—
    But twenty months and twa,
When an angel band frae the spirit land
    Cam' doon to tak' her awa' ;
And I tried wi' a' the strength I had,
    To say, " Thy will be done ;"
But I thocht my heart would break in twa
    When they laid her in the grun'.

I stood at the heid o' her wee bit grave,
    And her mither was by my side,
And her breist was heavin' up and doon
    Wi' grief that she couldna hide ;
And aye, as she lean'd her arm on mine,
    I could feel her tremblin' sair,

And her wailin' sabs sank mair deep in my heart
    Than e'en the minister's prayer.

I've aften thocht that the saddest sound
    That ony ane can hear,
Is heard when standin' by a grave,
    Wi' a' the mourners near,
And the coffin is lower'd to its resting place
    And frae your sicht is hid—
That waefu' sound which the dull earth mak's
    When it fa's on the coffin lid.

But it never seem'd sae sad to me
    As it did upon that day,
When our wee pet lamb that we lo'ed sae weel
    Was laid underneath the clay ;
And her mither shuddered afresh at the sound,
    And her grief burst forth anew,
And she cried, " that's the last o' our bonnie bairn ;
    We've nae wee Jeanie noo.

" The last, did I say, no not the last,
    For a hope to us is given,
Though we see our bairn nae mair on earth,
    That we'll meet her again in Heaven ;
And, husband, winna we baith be glad
    To meet wi' her again ?"
I couldna answer her just then,
    But I thocht I wud be fain,

I ken it's wrang to mourn for them
   That the Lord has ta'en awa';
But we're unco weak and unco frail,
   When misfortunes on us fa'.
God guide us a' and gie us grace—
   And mickle grace they need
That hae lo'ed a bairn as I lo'ed her,
   And that bairn lying deid.

The Last Fareweel.

[Lines written on the death of my Brother-in-Law, A. McIntyre.]

My lease o' life is nearly run, I ken I'm deein' noo ;
It canna be much langer ere I hae to pairt wi' you.
I feel my end is drawin' near, but that brings me nae pain,
Unless the thochts o' leaving you within the warld alane.

I'm glad my reason still remains to tak' fareweel o' thee—
In a' our trials you hae been a guid, guid wife to me ;
Be it your comfort when I'm gane to think I lo'ed ye weel,
An' ne'er had ony fau'ts to you, ye've aye been true an' leal.

Then dinna greet, my bonnie doo, as if your heart wud
    break,
It mak's me laith to leave the warld if only for your sake ;
I ken ye'll hae an unco fecht, ye'll hae to struggle sair,
A puir man's widow meets wi' much that's geyin' hard to
    bear.

But ye maun put your trust in Him wi' whom my peace is
    made,
An' then let come or gang what will you needna be afraid.
He mak's the wind blaw saft at nicht to lammies on the lea,
An' dinna doubt but what He'll tak far greater care o' thee.

It pleased the Lord to tak' frae us our bonnie bairnies twa,
An' weel I ken ye miss'd them sair when they were ta'en awa;
But Providence sustained you then, an' sae it will do noo—
If ye'll be guided by God's grace He'll bring you safely thro'.

I aften think aboot our bairns, (I'll sune be wi' them noo),
I dreamt a weesyne that they baith cam' back to me an' you.
Wee Allie took my han' in his, his een shone clear an' bricht.
An' Isa whispered in my ear "*you're gaun wi' us the nicht:*

"We'll tak you, faither, to a place that's free frae earthly
    care,
An' things that cause you trouble here will never vex you
    mair;
There's naethin' there that gangs ajee, there's nocht that can
    annoy,
It's a' a roun' o' endless bliss, an' happiness, an' joy."

I tauld them I wud gang wi' them, an' O! but they were
    glad;
But when I turn'd around an' saw you sittin' there sae sad,
The thochts o' what you yet micht dree before me quickly
    past,
An' I said I wudna leave you yet, my first luve an' my last.

There's somethin' pu'in' at my heart, I canna tell ye mair,
Wheesht, hinny, O! be comforted, you maunna greet sae
    sair;
Compose yoursel' an' try an' say the Lord's ain will be dune—
That's richt, we'll no be pairted lang, we'll sune meet up
    aboon.

Noo put your arms around my neck an' kiss me ere I dee ;
It is the last ye'll ever get upon this earth frae me.
I feel the pressure o' your lips, but canna see yoursel',
I hear Christ sayin', "Come awa"—fareweel, God bless you,
    Bell.

The Widow's Wail.

He's awa, he's awa to the "land o' the leal,"
　Frae this world o' sorrow and pain,
And it tried me sair to say fareweel
　When he left me a' alane,
But in my inmost heart I feel
　That my loss has been his gain.

He's awa, he's awa, and he winna come back,
　And my een wi' tears are dim,
And my heart is sometimes like to break
　That I canna gang to him.
I ken its wrang, but I'm frail and weak,
　And the future, whiles, looks grim.

He's awa, he's awa where I ken he'll meet
　Wi' our bonnie bairnies three,
And aften in their unions sweet,
　They will kindly talk o' me,
And speak o' a time that's coming yet,
　When we'll a' united be.

O Thou who art the widow's friend,
　Her comfort, hope and stay !
Thy counsel still unto me lend,
　Watch o'er me day by day,
And guide me on unto the end
　Of life's lang weary way.

Not Lost but Gone Before.

ON THE DEATH OF MY CHILD.

We've nae wee Lily noo, Maggie,
    We've nae wee Lily noo ;
Death's laid his cauld, damp, icy han'
    Upon her bonnie broo.
That broo whaur gowden ringlets play'd,
    Aboon her een o' blue.

'Twas destined sae to be, Maggie,
    'Twas destined sae to be,
That God should tak' awa' the gift
    He gied to you and me ;
'Twas hard to part wi't; sorrow's aye
    A bitter thing to dree.

She looked some like yoursel, Maggie,
    She looked some like yoursel ;
How much I lo'ed her nane but He
    Wha kens our hearts can tell.
We will not murmur at His will,
    He doeth all things well.

We'll miss her unco sair, Maggie,
    We'll miss her unco sair ;
But she has gane whaur grief and pain
    Will never reach her mair—
Whaur flowerets bloom and shed perfume
    In Heaven's garden fair.

We will not mourn her noo, Maggie,
　We will not mourn her noo ;
She isna lost but gane before—
　Just hidden frae our view ;
She's better aff than she could be,
　Were she still here wi' you.

We'll meet wi' her again, Maggie,
　We'll meet wi' her again,
When we hae passed thro' death's dark vale,
　And crossed o'er Jordan's plain ;
'Mang ither lammies in Christ's fauld
　We'll see our ain wee wean.

Scotland.

(Read Before the St. Andrew's Society, Hamilton.)

Hail, Scotland ! land o' mickle fame,
Where a' my forbears found a hame,
Where poets, sages and divines,
In pleasant places cast their lines—
Where honor, truth and worth are found,
And every " neuk" is " hallowed ground."
Land o' my sires ! tho' far away,
I greet thee on St. Andrew's Day.

I'm aye Canadian, a' the year,
Until Saint Andrew's Day draws near,
And then the Scotch blood fires my veins—
Auld Scotland the ascendant gains,
And vividly before my min'
Comes back the days o' Auld Lang Syne ;
When I by Kelvin's streams hae roved,
To dream and muse on things I loved—
Or wandered doon by Scotston Wood,
And there at eve enchanted stood
To hear the blackbird trill his lays,
And sing his evening sang o' praise,
Just ere the sun had sunk to rest
In that dear land he loves the best.

Leeze me ! on thee, Auld Scotland, dear,
Tho' parted four-and-twenty year,

Thy memory is as fresh and green
As tho' I'd left you but yestreen ;
And if I'd live a hunder year,
To me ye'd aye be just as dear.

Wha wadna love that mountain land.
Where Bruce and Wallace drew the brand
That first gave freedom to her sons,
And made their mem'ries hallow'd ones ?
Wha wadna love ilk flowery dell,
O'er which Scott threw his magic spell,
Where poesy enraptured reigns,
And sweetly sings in Doric strains?
Wha wadna love the land which gave
To Truth sae mony martyrs brave,
That didna fear to draw their sword
To fecht the battles o' the Lord,—
Wha for their conscience boldly stood,
Drenched to the very knees in blood,
And fearless shed their ain that we,
Their sons, should be forever free
To worship God, by nicht or day,
As our ain conscience points the way?
Wha wadna love its hills and dales,
Its blooming haughs and fertile vales,
Its broomy knowes and heath-clad fells,
The sweet sound o' its Sabbath bells,
Its grand auld kirks and worthy men,
Its martyrs' cairns on hill and glen,
Its bonnie, blooming, black-e'ed queans—

Ilk ane o' them like "Jeanie Deans;"
Its bards wha sang o' bonnets blue,
Its pibrochs, plaids, and mountain dew?—
A recreant loon that Scot must be
Wha disna love and honor thee.

My country! on thy shrine I lay
A heart that beats as true this day
As when I said fareweel to thee,
To follow fortune o'er the sea.

Thou ither Scotland unto me,
Dear as adopted land can be,
Fair Canada! for thee I feel
A deep heart-interest in thy weal.
Altho' thou hast not gi'en them birth,
The dearest anes to me on earth
Have found a grave upon thy soil,
To rest frae a' their cares and toil.
O may thy sons and daughters fair
A robe of truth and virtue wear!
Be they the guardians of thy fame,
And earn for thee an honor'd name
Among the nations of the earth
For valor, justice, truth, and worth.
Long may thy banners proudly wave
O'er freeborn maids and patriots brave!
And sparkling on their silken sheen
Like brilliants, may these words be seen,
(When to the breeze they are unfurl'd)—
"PEACE AND GOOD-WILL TO ALL THE WORLD!"

Remember the Poor.

(Respectfully dedicated to the Members of St. Andrew's Society, Hamilton.)

"Poor, naked wretches, wheresoe'er you are, that bide the pelting of this pitiless storm, how shall your houseless heads and unfed sides, your loop'd and window'd raggedness, defend you from seasons such as these."—SHAKSPEARE.

THE simmer days are past an' gane,
   An' a' their beauty's fled ;
The flowers that bloom'd sae fresh an' fair
   Are wither'd now an' dead.
Auld winter has come roun' ance mair,
   Wi' sleet, an' cauld, an' rain,
An' frost an' snaw will reign supreme
   For twa-three months again.

I'll no misca' the winter time,
   Altho' its blasts are keen,
An' snaw-drifts lie whaur shortly since
   The buddin' flowers were seen ;
For ilka season has its joys
   An' pleasures o' its ain,
An' Chris'mas comes in winter time
   To cheer our hearts again.

But when I think upon the puir,
   My heart is wae an' sad ;
Nae pleasure does it bring to them—
   Half-fed an' no half-clad.

God help them a' whaure'er they be,
    For mickle help they need
That hae nae siller in their pouch,
    Nor house aboon their heid.

O ! mony are the ills, I trow,
    That puir folk hae to dree,
An' bitter are the pangs they thole
    Thro' want an' poverty.
Nae wonder, then, they rise sometimes,
    An' tak' what's been denied,—
A starvin' wife an' twa-three weans
    Are unco sair to bide.

Ye wha in cosie parlors sit
    Beside a cheerfu' fire,
Wi' ilka thing aroun' ye that
    Your wishes can desire,
Think what a difference there is
    Between your state an' theirs :
You've nocht but joys on every han'—
    Their life is fu' o' cares.

Then dinna hoard your siller up,
    An' keep't frae being seen ;
But mak' guid use o' a' the gifts
    That God to you has gi'en.
Gae forth amang the streets an' lanes,
    An' do whate'er you can
To mak' the puir folks' sufferings less,
    An' help your fellow-man.

An' bear the Golden Rule in min',
   An' act upon it, too,
Aye do to ithers as you would
   Hae ithers do to you.
You'll naething lose tho' ye to them
   Some little help afford ;
For them wha gi'es unto the puir,
   Is lendin' to the Lord.

The Gathering of the Clans.

(Respectfully dedicated to the Members of the St. Andrew's
Society, of Hamilton.)

" Wat ye wha's a coming ? "

THE birthday o' the Queen's coming :
The games upon the green's coming ;
    O'er hill and dale
    And muir and vale
The clans will a' be seen coming.

There's mony men o' rank coming ;
The Laird o' Athol Bank's coming :
    Macnab, Macraw,
    And Service, wha
Aye fills a muckle bank's coming.

Muir, Murray and McLean's coming ;
Buchanan, Binny, Baine's coming ;
    The Browns and Hopes,
    McKays, Dunlops,
And a' their wives and weans coming.

The Frazers, ane and a's, coming ;
The Campbells, great and sma's, coming ;
    McKenzies, Kerrs,
    The Findlays, Blairs,
The Craigies, Harveys, Law's coming.

The Sutherland's great clan's coming,
And Osborne in the van's coming,
    The Watsons true,
    Brave Angus, too,
And Dawson and his Nan's coming.

McPherson and McNeil's coming,
And Roy, a royal chiel's, coming ;
    And wi' the lave
    There's mony a brave
Descendant o' Lochiel coming.

Bruce, Hutchison and Bell's coming ;
And Leggat (Mat. himsel's) coming ;
    And o'er the mead
    The Hendries lead
Mair men than I can tell, coming.

Brave chiels frae Tweed and Tay's coming;
Braw lads frae Clyde and Spey's coming,
    And mony a lass,
    Frae hill and pass,
Thinks fondly o' that day coming.

Edina's bairns are a' coming,
And Aberdeen awa's coming ;
    And lads frae Doon
    And Mungo's toon,
And "queer folk frae the Shaws" coming.

Auld pawky Adam Glen's coming,
The Lass o' Hawthornden's coming,

And Mistress Jean
Declared yestreen
That she and auld Cockpen's coming.

There's strapping lads frae Fife coming,
Neil Gow and his guid wife's coming,
And Heather Jock,
And Paisley folk,
Expanding wi' new life's, coming.

There's Eastwoods, Stewarts, Mack's coming,
And Robertsons and Jack's coming.
St. Andrew's sent
A muckle tent,
And wi' it Dannie Black's coming.

There's Skinners, Reids and Tait's coming,
McGiverin, the great's, coming,
There's ne'er a Scot
In a' the lot,
But's proud to be his mate, coming.

Our auld Saint will look doon, then,
On ilka ane aroun', then ;
Weel pleased he'll be
His bairns to see,
Frae country and frae toon, then.

Dundurn ! thy towers will ring, then ;
Our cares will a' tak' wing then ;
The pipes will play,
And blythe and gay
We'll dance the Highland fling, then.

Auld Scotia's Games.

AULD Scotia's games! Auld Scotia's games
  I like to see them a':
They bring thegither buirdly chiels,
  And bonnie lasses braw;
They wile us frae our cares at times,
  And frae our cosy hames;
It's pleasant whiles to spend a day
  To see Auld Scotia's games.

It's grand to see the caber tossed,
  Or watch them throw the quoit;
And when the "Gillie Callum's" danced,
  It fills us wi' delight.
It cheers the heart and fires the bluid
  To dance a blythe Strathspey
Wi' some young sonsie queen wha's een
  Are black as ony slae,

It brings our native hills and dales
  And glens again around',
To see the pipers in their kilts
  Gaun marchin' up and doon;
And hear them play some warlike air,
  Or some auld cantie spring,
Till lads and lasses loup like daft,
  And dance the Highland fling.

Oh, Canada ! I lo'e ye weel !
Altho' nae son o' thine,
Within thy wide domain their beats
Nae truer heart than mine ;
But when a day like this comes roun',
Auld Scotia has her claims :
The thistle aye comes uppermost—
I gang to see the games !

Peter Fraser, Esq.

(Sung at a supper given him by the St. Andrew's Society, Hamilton, Ontario.)

———

AIR—"*My Mither Mend't my Auld Breeks.*"

———

THERE's some wha sing o' Lords and Dukes,
    And men like Julius Cæsar;
I sing an honest, worthy man—
    His name is Peter Fraser.
Altho' he isna what ye ca'
    Ane o' these titled gentry,
He's been a credit to us a'—
    An honor to his country.

      A fig for Peers and Potentates,
        Or ony King or Kaiser;
      We've men amang us truly great,
        And ane is Peter Fraser.

When Nature thought she'd mak' a man
    That never wud disgrace her,
She gaed awa' to Inverness—
    That queer, auld-fashioned place, sir—

And lang she wrought baith night and day
   Ere she got ane to please her ;
At length (o' guid auld Hieland clay)
   She made up Peter Fraser.

     Then a fig for Peers and Potentates, &c.

How well she's done her handiwork
   His actions aye ha'e shown us ;
For deeds speak louder far than words,
   And muckle guid he's done us.
If merit meets wi' due respect,
   Then Peter will get plenty ;
There's no ae man deserves it mair
   In nineteen out o' twenty.

     Then a fig for Peers and Potentates, &c.

The Highland bluid that warms his veins,
   Frae sires he did inherit,
Wha hardly kent what failure meant,
   Sae dauntless was their spirit ;
And men wha storm'd Quebec wi' Wolfe,
   Or wi' Ross climb'd the glaciers,
Had hearts made out o' just such stuff
   As that o' Peter Fraser's.

     Then a fig for Peers and Potentates, &c.

Saint Andrew's sons will miss him sair
   Whene'er he leaves the city,

For he has always foremost been
  Upon the path of duty ;
And mony a puir but honest Scot
  By him has been befriended—
His heart was open to their wants,
  His hand was aye extended.

      Then a fig for Peers and Potentates, &c.

Now, Peter, lad, we're unco sad,
  And sairly does it grieve us,
To think that you and your guid wife
  Are gaun awa' to leave us ;
But when you get to Inverness,
  She aften will remind ye,
While ye on " Clach-na-cudin "* sit,
  O' friends you left behind ye.

    While wand'ring by the banks o' Ness,
      Amang the blooming heather,
    Ye'll think on mony happy nights
      That we ha'e spent thegither.

---

* Clach-na-cudin ; literally, the Stone of the Tub—a famous old stone in the High Street of Inverness, where, in days gone by, when the now thriving and fashionable capital of the Scottish Highlands was a mere fishing " Clachan," the Highland maidens were wont to rest with their tubs, (and, of course, meet their sweethearts), on the way to or from "washing" in the Ness. No visitor to Inverness, with any regard for the sacred things of auld lang syne, fails to sit on Clach-na-cudin.

May naething happen you or her
   Will gi'e ye cause for grievin' ;
May fortune, friends, and a' that's guid,
   Be yours as lang's ye're leivin' ;
May Heaven send you o' its gifts
   It's very choicest treasures,
And bless your wife, and hae a care
   O'er a' the little Frasers.

     Then, lads, around the jorum pass,
       And dinna scrimp the measure ;
      And fill a cup, and toast it up
       To worthy Peter Fraser.

The Auld Scotchman's Welcome to his First Fit.

A GUID New Year unto ye a',
   An' mony may ye see ;
An' as ilk ither ane comes roun',
   Mair happy may ye be.
I'm proud that ye've first fitted me,
   I'm glad to see you here ;
An' sae I wish you a' again,
   Anither guid New Year.

But dinna stan' outside the door,
   But come your wa's in ben ;
Gudewife, put on a weel faur'd mutch,
   An' bring the " Tappit Hen."
Let's hae a drap o' " mountain dew,"
   Be happy while ye 're here ;
Wha kens gin we may ever see,
   Anither guid New Year ?

Sit doon my frien's aroun' the fire,
   An' keep the cauld awa' :
Our auld gudewife 'll soon be here,
   Wi' somethin' for us a'.
An' thankfu' let us be to Him,
   Wha keeps us hale an' fier ;
For mony blessin's we've received,
   An' mony a guid New Year.

Now ye maun hae a taste frae me,
  To thaw ye're frozen mou';
There's no' much wrang if ance a year,
  We get a "wee thocht" fou.
Here's wishin' weel to ane an' a,'
  That's roun' aboot me here;
An' may we a' be spared to see,
  Anither guid New Year.

There's Mony a Slip 'Twixt the Cup an' the Lip.

THERE's mony a slip 'twixt the cup an' the lip,
  That's gey weel understood,
But there far mair slips when the cup to the lips
  Gangs oftener than it shou'd.
" When the wine is in then the wit is out,"
  Is a saying auld an' true ;
Then tak' guid care o' what you're aboot,
  Or else ye may dearly rue.

The joys ye buy at the festive board
  Aft cost ye far o'er dear,
The frien's that ye shake han's wi' there,
  · Are seldom 'ere sincere.
I've heerd folk tell that the Deil himsel'
  Thraw's glamor o'er the wine,
An' he draws aroun' ye its witchin' spell,
  Till ye tint your peace o' mind.

Then he lures ye on frae bad to waür
  Till ye come to some bad en',
He breaks the hearts o' wives and weans,
  An' he ruins the saul's o' men.
Then, brithren a', before ye fa'
  I rede ye to beware
An' tak' guid heed that ye dinna tread
  On the drunkard's path nae mair,

They'll Hae Lang Spoons that'll Sup wi' the Deil.

THEY'LL hae geyin lang spoons that'll sup wi' the Deil,
 If they e'er want to come ony speed,
For I'm tauld that his elbow's as supple's an eel,
 An' he's just like a gled in his greed ;
Since the day he was seen in a serpentine shape,
 He's been kenn'd for an auld-fashioned chiel,
An' he's ready for a' things, his mouth's aye agape
 Like the mouth o' a fisherman's creel.

But yet for a' that there is seldom a feast
 That tak's place whaur he isna a guest :
He dines wi' the statesman, he dines wi' the priest,
 Whichever ane suits him the best.
It's a wonderfu' thing, let him gang whaur he likes,
 He's maistly aye sure o' a meal,
An' as happy's a bee when it bums roun' its byke,
 When he's pleased, is his worship the Deil.

He's aye on the glaum, baith by nicht an' by day,
 An' lays han's on a' he can get ;
He's isna particular what comes in his way—
 It's a' fish that gangs into his net ;
He's fond o' a dish made o' " wranged orphans' tears,"
 Them wha gar the tears flow he likes weel,
But "birds o' a feather are fond o' each ither,"
 (Put that flea in your lug, Maister Deil.)

If there's naething that's made that has been made in vain.
　Then the Deil maun be usefu' at times :
The ministers tell us, again and again,
　That he's sent as a scourge for our crimes.
Ye wha glory in dinin' upon feasts o' sin,
　There is ae thing I'd hae you mind weel :
Ye'll be early sat doon, and ye'll hae a lang spoon,
　If ye sup sowp about with the Deil.

The Champion Drunkard of Ontario

THE de'il tak' you, James Livingstone,
  Ye've cost the toon a heap o' siller,
Ye're drinkin' a' the time, an' yet
  Ye're aye as dry as ony miller.

Day after day, week after week,
  Month after month, ye never tire ;
I canna see how you can haud
  Sic quantities o' "liquid fire."

There's some can tak' a drap at times,
  An' keep within the bounds o' reason ;
But you are no' content wi' that,
  Ye're at it in an' out o' season.

Want it wha likes, ye're bound to hae 't,
  As lang as ye can beg or borrow ;
Ye've drank enough to droon a toon
  As big as Sodom or Gomorrah.

If whiskey fill'd our lakes, then ye
  Adown your throat would keep it pourin',
Until ye drank Ontario dry
  An' drain'd Lake Erie an' Lake Huron.

Twa hunder' times, aye mair than that,
  Ye've been in "Castle Milne"* for drinkin';
Had ye been treated to the "Cat,"†
  Ye'd no be there sae aft, I'm thinkin'.

Its unco hard that worthy folk,
  Guid honest, decent workin' chiels,
Should be compell'd to keep an' feed
  A set o' drucken ne'er-do-weels.

The maist o' things ha'e got an end,
  (A puddin' we are tauld has twa ;)
But much I doot ye'll never quat
  The whiskey till ye're ta'en awa'.

I think sometimes, an' ye maun own
  That the conclusion is a just one,
If you don't stop ye'll dee o' what
  Is ca'd spontaneous combustion.

An' when ye're lyin' wi' the deid,
  An' dune wi' drinkin' in this warl',
Your epitaph like this will read,
  Here lies a worn-oot whiskey barrel.

---

* Castle Milne, Hamilton Jail.
† Cat-o'-nine-tails.

Hamilton.

In free and fair Ontario the summer sun looks down,
On many a goodly city and on many a thriving town ;
But in our wide Dominion there is not a single one
That has a better claim to fame than that of Hamilton.

Her white-winged messengers of trade sail over lake and sea,
And north and south and east and west their flags are flying
    free ;
While through her midst, with fiery breath, like lightning in
    its course,
And bearing commerce in its train, there speeds the iron
    horse.

The busy hum of industry upon her streets is heard,
And Science vies with Art, and Toil brings home a fair
    reward ;
Her artizans have earned a place upon the scroll of fame,
And Europe's sons have learned to pay respect unto her
    name. ·

Her merchants in their dealings have a reputation won
For honor and integrity that is excelled by none.
At home, abroad, their enterprise and energy we trace ;
Wherever sterling worth ranks high they hold an honor'd
    place.

We have no gorgeous palaces, no airy cloud-capp'd tow'rs,
No halls of regal state within this "Hamilton of ours;"
But we have homes where virtue reigns, and peace and
  comfort dwell,
And churches filled with worshippers when sounds the
  Sabbath bell.

No fairer maids tread God's green earth than Hamilton can
  boast—
Though fair their forms, it is not that for which we prize them
  most;
It is their loveliness of mind wherein their merit lies,
And modest, unassuming worth finds homage in our eyes.

And should their homes endanger'd be, our maidens need
  not fear,
In their defence we well can trust each gallant volunteer.
The trust we have reposed in them is sacred to them all—
" Aye ready," are they when they hear the bugle's stirring
  call.

Thy sons and daughters, Hamilton, may well feel proud of
  thee,
Thy record in the past is good, great will thy future be;
Within this glorious land of ours (and there's no land more
  blest,)
There's many a goodly city, but I love our own the best.

Fireside Memories.

In the long ago, in the happy days
    When you and I were young,
We wandered o'er the sunny braes,
    Where clustering hazels hung ;
We gathered sloes and berries red,
    Where the crystal streamlets flow,
And the lark sung gaily o'er our head,
    In the happy long ago.

In the happy days, in the long ago
    When we sat 'neath the birchen tree,
And the sun shone down on your hair so brown,
    And your eyes looked love to me ;
The throstle piped in joy to his mate,
    When, in accents soft and low,
You whisper'd me my bride you'd be
    In the happy long ago.

Your hair is tinged with silver now,
    And we both are growing old,
But the love we pledged each other then
    Has never since grown cold ;
Our summer is past, and autumn has come—
    It will soon be winter's snow,
But my heart beats true as it did to you
    In the happy long ago.

Ah ! wife, the time will come when we
  In the churchyard will be laid,
And the friends that loved us when in life
  Will forget us when we're dead ;
May we lie together side by side
  Till the angel's trump shall blow,
And the Christ has come who died for us
  In the long, long, long ago.

The Laborer's Return.

FOUR little feet
Coming down the street,
Flying along as if running a " heat ;"
Two happy faces beaming with joy,
One little girl and one little boy.
She with her bright eyes comes bounding along—
He with his rosy cheeks, healthy and strong,
Laughing and shouting as onward they come
To welcome their father from work coming home ;
Two little mouths are held up for a kiss,
Causing a heart-thrill, a feeling of bliss—
What joy in the world is equal to this?

Their mother keeps watch at the cottage door,
And her heart with love it is running o'er ;
Well pleased, she sees, looking down the street,
That her husband seems happy their children to meet.
As he raises the youngest one up in his arms
(Its face all glowing with Nature's charms),
In those great round arms of his, so strong,
While they merrily chat to him coming along.
And he lists to the talk of his children twain,
Overjoyed to be with them at evening again,
And the face of their mother beams bright with a smile,
As she welcomes her husband come back from his toil.

He enters the house and sits down in his chair,
And says, while they gather around him there :

" This is the bank where my wealth is stored,
And none has a treasure that's more adored."
Then he turns to the table and rev'rently says :
" All Gracious Father, to Thee be the praise,
For food, and for raiment, and covering, we
Desire to be thankful, O Lord, unto Thee,
For health and each blessing we daily enjoy,
And for that peace of mind there is naught can destroy.
Accept of our thanks, Lord, again and again,
And pardon our sins for Thy Son's sake, Amen."

Grace ended, his wife gaily serves out the tea,
And a sweet little, blithe little woman is she,
With his girl beside him, and his boy on his knee,
No king in the world is prouder than he.
While he lists to their prattle the meal passes by,
An hour more for playing, and their bed-time draws nigh.
        And the four little feet,
        That ran down the street,
Are weary and tired now, and worn out complete.
Then their mother unrobes them and puts them to bed,
(But not until after their prayers have been said),
In a few minutes after there comes a " wee cheep,"
" Dust tiss us once more 'Pa, an' we go to seep."
He enters their room and he bends down his head,
And says, while he looks at them nestling in bed,
" God keep you my children, all safe and all right,
Now, then, both of you kiss me," "good night, Pa," "dood nite."

Respect the Dead.

ON THE DESECRATION OF GRAVES IN CEMETERIES.

Give something to the dead.   Give what?   Respect.—KNOWLES.

SHAME on the sacrilegious wretch
    Would pluck the heart-gifts from a grave,
And, in mere wantonness, destroy
    Those tributes which affection gave !

Gave to the memory of those
    Who from this earth have passed away ;
Are they not records which denote
    Our love for them knows no decay?

The Widow sows flowers on the grave
    Of him who loved her well in life ;
The Husband pays respect through them
    To her who was his faithful wife.

The Orphan, weeping, kneels beside
    The grave that holds her parents dear,
And puts "a sweet remembrance" there,
    And waters it with many a tear.

Yon maiden with the pensive brow,
    Mourns one she knew who loved her well ;
And, bending o'er his grave at eve,
    She strews the plaintive *immortelle.*

Those places sacred are to them,
  Whatever they may be to you ;
And were you just and pure in heart,
  You would hold them in reverence, too.

That flower, so rudely torn apart,
  A loving Mother's hand placed there,
In memory of a darling child,
  She watched and nursed with tender care.

But all her care availed her naught—
  Death took her bonny blue-eyed boy—
That spot she cherishes so dear
  Would you maliciously destroy ?

Have you no thought—care you for naught—
  Is every spark of feeling fled,
That thus you basely desecrate
  Those sacred " dwellings of the dead " ?

" Flowers are God's children," and where'er
  Love may have placed them, let them stand ;
Nor with unhallowed hands profane
  Those emblems of the " Better Land."

The Engine Driver.

(*Respectfully dedicated to the Engine Drivers on the Great Western
Railway of Canada.*)

RATTLE along, my Iron Steed,
So lithe of limb and free;
There's somebody fifty miles away
That is wishing God speed to thee.
There's somebody sits in the cot by the track
Beguiling the time with a song,
Whose eyes will sparkle with pure delight
When she sees thee come bounding along.
Then merrily, cheerily rattle along,
Thy sinews of steel are tough and strong.

Rattle along, my Iron Steed,
Merrily over the rail;
Thy course is fleeter and swifter far
Than a ship before the gale;
The eagle swooping down on its prey
Cannot cope with thee in speed;
The mountain stag on his native hills
Is no match for thee, my steed.
Then merrily, cheerily rattle along,
Thy sinews of steel are tough and strong.

Now, now thy breathing quicker comes,
My hand is on thy rein;

Step out, my beauty, and falter not,
    Till ye carry me home again,—
For Maggie she sits in the little porch
    Along with our children three,
And I know they are looking with longing eyes,
    And watching for you and me.
Then merrily, cheerily rattle along,
Thy sinews of steel are tough and strong.

Well done, well done ! we are nearing home,
    And my heart is beating fast :
One minute more and we'll round the curve—
    There's the signal post at last !
Nay, pause not yet, but rattle along,
    With cheerful merry birr,
The shriek from thy brazen throat will sound
    Like music sweet to her.
Then merrily, cheerily rattle along,
Thy sinews of steel are tough and strong.

Guessed I not right? See, there she is,
    Outside the cottage door,
And the ribbon fluttering in her hair
    Is a welcome semaphore.
Lord love my babe, how it laughs and crows,
    And keeps jumping upon her knee ;
While Willie and Annie are out on the stile,
    Both waving their hands to me.
Then merrily, cheerily rattle along,
Thy sinews of steel are tough and strong.

God bless you, my wife ! now halt, my steed,
   Our labor has not been vain ;
There's many a woman as well as she
   Will bless thy coming again.
There's many a one will be glad to-night,
   And some that will wish God speed
To the men who bring them such precious freight,
   And who ruleth the Iron Steed.
Now rest thee, my steed, our labor is done,
And to-morrow again we'll be up with the sun.

A Sabbath Morn's Reverie.

(Composed whilst beholding the sun rise near the beautiful residence of John Brown, Esq., at five o'clock in the morning, May 25th 1873.)

BLESS God for this holy sabbath morn,
    While the robins their early matins are singing,
And the maples are spreading their foliage of green,
    And the air with a tremulous joy is ringing!
All Nature, in its various ways,
Is sending forth its Maker's praise.

The city lies hush'd in a holy calm,
    While the sun is shedding his beams abroad,
And everything seems as fresh and pure
    As it was when it came from the hands of God.
Like a mirror of silver shines the Bay—
As clear and as bright as the Milky Way.

Its great heart-throbs are silent and still—
    Not a ruffle appears to disturb its breast;
As I gaze on it from the brow of the hill,
    It seems to add to the placid rest
Of this peaceful morn. What a pleasure and bliss
If all our morns were a Sabbath like this!

Like this! It seems a foretaste of the time
    Which the Lord hath promised to us will be given
When His will shall be done upon this earth
    As it is already done in Heaven.
O Lord, list the prayer of a heart sincere.
Save all who abide in the city here!

Little Lizzie.

LITTLE Lizzie, bright and fair ;
Lizzie with the golden hair ;
Eyes that beam with life and love—
Sweet wee totum, cooing dove.
Winsome, gleesome, prattling pet,
Rosebud, snowdrop, violet,
Zephyr, wafting here and there—
Lizzie with the golden hair.

Teasing, pleasing, laughing thing,
Joyous as a bird in Spring ;
Brooklets, singing as they run,
Glancing, dancing in the sun,
Are not merrier than thou art :
Bless thy gentle loving heart ;
Heaven keep thee in its care—
Darling, with the golden hair.

Rain.

RAIN, rain, welcome again !
Long have we wished for thee, wished but in vain ;
Now thou art come with thy blessings again,
Glad welcome we give thee, thou heart-cheering rain.

Welcome to flow'rets long drooping their heads,
Welcome to streams nearly dry in their beds,
Welcome to forest and mountain and plain,
Welcome, thrice welcome, thou swift-falling rain.

Welcome to herds on the parched mountain's brow,
Welcome to flocks in the valley below,
Welcome to meadow and orchard and grain,
Everything's singing thy welcome again.

Welcome art thou to the tired sons of toil,
Lighting our faces again with a smile,
Cooling the fever that burns in our brain,
A thousand times welcome, thou life-giving rain.

Our Bonnie Bay.

O BRIGHTLY shines the summer sun
　　Upon our bonnie bay !
Our little bark at anchor rides
　　And chafes to get away.
The crystal wavelets kiss her prow,
　　And glance along her side ;
Ontario woos her with its smiles,
　　As lover woos his bride,
　　　　Then go with me, my winsome quean,
　　　　　And spend the summer day—
　　　　Where health is found and joys abound—
　　　　　Upon our bonnie bay.

The breeze that fills our swelling sail
　　Will waft us gaily on,
Where little Islets, green and fair,
　　Lie basking in the sun.
The zephyrs cool will fan thy brow,
　　And through thy tresses play ;
Thy cheek will gain a richer hue
　　Upon our bonnie bay.
　　　　Then go with me, my winsome quean,
　　　　　And spend the summer day—
　　　　Where health is found and joys abound—
　　　　　Upon our bonnie bay.

O brightly shines the summer sun
  On forest, hill and dale !
And from the woodlands comes the breath
  Of many a perfumed vale.
All nature wears its richest garb,
  To lure you forth to day ;
But nowhere does it look so sweet
  As round our bonnie bay.
      Then go with me, my winsome quean,
        And spend the summer day—
      Where health is found and joys abound—
        Upon our bonnie bay.

Impromptu,

ON SEEING A MAGNIFICENT BUFFALO'S HEAD PACKED FOR TRANS-
PORTATION TO EUROPE.

GREAT monarch of the Western Prairie, hail!
  Shorn of thy strength, thy head lies prostrate—low;
Time was, when thou wert swift and sure of foot,
  And strong of heart and limb—brave Buffalo.

Was it a rifle-bullet pierced thy breast—
  Or feathered shaft from painted Redskin's bow?
Or did some "brave," more daring than the rest,
  Get thee entangled in the strong lasso?

Oft thou has sported at the even-tide,
  With thy loved mate, beside some glassy stream;
Vaulting and coursing with a Bison's pride,
  When life to thee was like a summer's dream.

Or pranced along the Prairie by her side,
  The maddest, merriest of the Bovine race;
Watching with jealous care thy dark-eyed bride,
  When danger threatened, and thy foes gave chase.

No more the grass will bend beneath thy tread;
  For thee the salt-lick spring may now run dry—
The herd no more will follow in thy lead;
  Forever's dimmed the flashing of thine eye.

Great chieftain of the plains ! with visage sage,
    (Save when in am'rous mood, thou woo'd thy mate,)
Jove's thunderbolts were nothing to thy rage,
    Could'st thou but view thy present trunkless state.

Europa's sons will gaze on thee with dread,
    When thou art borne in safety o'er the brine ;
And look, perchance, upon thee as the " head"
    Of (not) the " *Allan*," but the " *Buffalo* line."

Mayhap they'll crack some jokes upon thy " *nut*,"
    There are but few will mourn thy overthrow ;
'Tis natural for men to make a *butt*
    Of " Lo, the poor Indian," and the Buffalo.

Spring Thoughts.

HAIL balmy spring !—all but the balm—the balm is all my
   eye,—
Thou com'st again, to deck the earth with rich and gorgeous
   dye ;
The Frost King's revelled long enough with all his icy train,
With gladsome hearts—just new thawed out—we welcome
   thee again.

The Winter's passing from us now, while you come right
   along.
And, like an honest shoemaker, the sun is *waxing* strong.
The " beautiful" is vanishing, the robins *try* to sing,
" Old Probabilities" declares that these are signs of Spring.

The brooks that were ice-bound are "loose," and gambol on
   their way,
As blythe as lambkins in a field upon a summer's day.
Frost jewels glitter in the sun and sparkle on the trees ;
The influenza still prevails and causes us to sneeze.

All nature looks more beautiful, the dry goods clerks begin
To titivate themselves again and barberize their chin ;
Their hair is parted carefully and smoothed is their cravats,
Their wide-awakes are laid aside for highfalutin' hats.

Our ladies—bless them one and all !—parade our thorough-
   fares,

And throw their sweetest smiles away and put on " gushing "
    airs.
Whene'er you see them float around like swallows on the wing,
Be sure that they are hunting up "tip-tilters"* for the Spring.

And who, that has a heart to love, would grudge a treble X—
Say once a month—to keep in tune those of the softer sex ?
Spring were no Spring were we without their cheery looks
    and smiles ;
Our homes would be the scene of feuds, domestic cares and
    broils.

Boys will be boys ! men will be men ! and o'er the whole
    world wide
Our women now are just the same as Eve when in her pride.
No doubt that Adam thought himself abused, you may depend,
When Eve first asked a V from him to buy a Grecian bend.

Our housemaids sweep our door-steps now; policemen on
    their " beat "
Are casting sheep's eyes here and there on almost every street ;
Our Aldermen are sleek and fat, and none the worse for wear,
And sip their Spring-brewed ale again, and give no thought
    to care.

Long live our Aldermen, say I, and may they " waddle" round,
And do whate'er within them lie to keep our taxes down ;
When at our doors, at early morn, the Tax Assessors ring,
With throbbing hearts we go to greet those " voices of the
    Spring."

---

*"Tip-tilters" are the latest style of ladies' bonnets.

The whitewash brushes are brought out, and men begin to
  frown
And say "sweet things" whene'er they hear of stove-pipes
  coming down ;
I've said a few myself, and drained the dregs of sorrow's cup,
When nailing bedroom carpets down, or putting stove-pipes up.

From out their lairs the Hurdy-gurdyists again go forth—
These sons of sunny Italy, they always travel north ;
With " Darwin Aboriginals,"† who cut the pigeon wing,
Our streets are made more lively by those harbingers of Spring.

The cuckoo's notes make glad the groves—in England—in
  the Spring ;
Canadians never hear, nor think, nor dream of such a thing ;
Our cuckoos are not musical ; the only notes we know
Are I. O. U.'s we sometimes give to Mr. So-and-so.

And when these notes are falling due, sad thoughts to us
  they bring,
If we—as is most likely—cannot meet them in the Spring !
I love the Spring with all my heart—who would not love
  what's grand ?
I love the cuckoo's notes as well, but not the notes-of-hand.

Tom Hood and Thomson sung of Spring, but then they
  knew their " biz;"
I will not bid it *hail* again—its hailed, and snowed, and *friz*,
Till I am sick and tired of it, and gladly would I bring
My mind to think that Winter's gone, and this, at last, is
  Spring !

---

† Monkeys.

To Wm. Durdan, and the Brethren of Hamilton Division, No. 133, B. of L. Engineers.

DEAR BROTHERS IN TOIL,
  I received your kind gift
Along with your flattering letter ;
  I was not aware I had ever done aught
By which I had made you my debtor.
  I value your gift—but I value much more
The spirit in which it was given ;
  To have the respect and esteem of our friends,
Is something that's always worth having.

May the great " Brotherhood," of which you're a part,
  Continue to prosper and flourish ;
The mottoes which you have adopted for it
  Long may you continue to cherish.
With Justice and Truth on your side, and the will
  To do what is right unto others,
Can't fail in the end to be crowned with success,
  And help to make all mankind Brothers.

'Tis pleasing to think when you're done with this world,
  That those dear ones you're leaving behind
Will receive the reward of your forethought and care
  From your Brothers, true-hearted and kind.

May * Burnfield and Morgan, and Torry look down
   From their home, in the leal-land above.
And bless those kind hearts, who first taught you the way
   To unite in this circle of love.

While running along on the railroad of life,
   Be kind and be just to your neighbours ;
And when your trip's ended, be sure you will gain
   A happy result from your labours.
When your fires have gone out, and your engine's laid up.
   And your whistle no longer is heard,
May you hear the glad words—" Faithful servants, well done ;
   Enter into the joy of thy Lord."

All three were killed while doing their duty.

* Westward, Ho !

HAMILTON TO THE RESCUE.

RISE fellow-men, up and be doing :
   Chicago unto you is crying ;
Her city is smoking in ruin,
   The fire-fiend around it is flying ;
There are thousands there destitute now,
   There are thousands are calling for bread,
There are thousands who ne'er dream'd of needing your help,
   Who have nowhere to lay down their head !

Give with a will, and give soon :
   Do not, oh ! do not delay ;
Remember, the evil they suffer from now
   May be ours yet at some future day ;
Sympathize with your deeds, not your words ;
   Give freely whatever is given ;
Charity's blessed, and from earth rises up
   Like a sweet-smelling incense to Heaven !

Up, Hamilton, then, and be doing :
   Chicago unto you is crying ;
Her city is smoking in ruin,
   The fire-fiend around it is flying ;
Come forward unto her relief,
   And help to dispel all her sorrow ;
She has pass'd through a night of great grief,
   Be it yours to make bright her to-morrow.

* Written the evening the city was busy in making up relief to send to Chicago.

Morning.

NIGHT lifts her mantle from the earth,
    The stars have gone away,
The cheerful songsters in the grove
    Salute the new-born day.

The little flowers, whose tiny cups
    Have all been filled with dew,
Now ope their eyes, in joyous glee,
    To see the sun burst through.

And far o'er hill and dale he spreads
    His genial beams abroad,
While everything in nature sends
    Its praises forth to God.

Tribute to Rosa D'Erina,

WELCOME Erin's Prima Donna,
  Greet her with a happy throng;
Welcome Erin's lute-toned minstrel,
  Erin's matchless Queen of Song.

Gems from many lands she brings us,
  Brilliants from the Muse's brain ;
Italy declares her peerless,
  Ma Belle France, and sunny Spain.

Sweet the lays of ancient Erin
  To our memory she recalls ;
Hark ! the harp again is sounding,
  As of yore thro' Tara's Halls.

While her strains of fairy music
  Fall on our enraptured ear,
Fancy brings the hallowed valleys
  Of our country to us near.

Every scene we loved in childhood,
  Which we looked upon with pride,
Rises, vision-like, before us,
  Floating over memory's tide.

There's the stile where sat dear Mary,
  On that shining summer morn ;

Sweet the sky-lark's song is ringing
 O'er the fields of waving corn.

Hark the bells of Shandon pealing,
 Ringing out with joyous glee;
While the autumn moon's revealing
 All the beauties of the Lea.

See the last Rose of the Summer
 Bending in the evening gale;
List the rippling of the waters
 In Avoca's lovely vale.

Welcome Erin's dark-eyed daughter,
 Greet her with a happy throng,
While in thought we cross the Ocean,
 To that land of love and song.

To Miss Maggie M——.

ROSE COTTAGE, HAMILTON.

"EVERY household has its angel."
  Maggie, darling, you are mine,—
Just as good and fair as any
  In the Eden-land divine.

"Every household has its angel."
  Would to heaven they had two,
If each one of them were only
  Half as good and kind as you.

Some there are who say that angels
  Long ago forsook the earth.
I deny it; none but angels
  Are possessed of half thy worth.

What is it makes women angels?
  Following out their Maker's plan—
Flitting here and there like sunbeams,
  Doing good where'er they can;

Watching o'er the bed of sickness,
  Sharing sorrows, care and grief—
Minist'ring to those who need it,
  Striving aye to bring relief.

Such thou art, and oh! may Heaven
  Blessings shower on thee and thine.
"All good angels keep and guard thee,"
  Maggie, darling, angel mine.

To Miss Annie Browne.

ON HER TWENTIETH BIRTHDAY.

DEAR NIECE, I got your little note
Informing me of what you thought,
Of drawing nearer to that state
Which all young ladies dread and hate.
And you I see are like the rest,
Not willing you should stand the test
Of letting all your charms decay,
Before you " throw yourself away."

I think you need not be afraid
Of turning out a " cross old maid ;"
E'en though your years have reached a score,
You'll keep at least a dozen more
Before you need to have a care,
Or think of dying in despair.
So don't sit down and cry and mope,
For while there's life, you know, there's hope.

I do not want you to delay,
Nor throw a single chance away ;
But if you have made up your mind,
To enter in at Hymen's shrine
As soon as you can get a beau,
That's willing with you there to go,

Then let me put you on a plan
To get at least a decent man.

Don't be a vain, affected prude,
Nor yet be forward, bold, or rude ;
A maiden can be gay and free,
And still possessed of modesty.
I'd rather see you kind and true,
And wise, in all your actions too ;
Let virtue form your leading part,
Be sure you wear it next your heart.
That is the brightest, purest gem,
That graces woman's diadem ;
O ne'er from virtue turn aside,
But let it be your constant guide,
Then whether you are maid or wife,
'Twill bring you happiness through life.
Ne'er play the silly coquette's part,
And trifle with an honest heart.
Of all vain fools they are the chief,
And well deserve to come to grief ;
But when you find a heart that's true,
That beats with honest love for you,
Then take your chance among the rest,
(It's but a lottery at the best.)
There's many that are married now
Would give the world to be like you.
Some find their path, with roses strewed,
And they of course pronounce it good ;
While others, from the time they're wed,

On thorns and thistles make their bed ;
O may the first of these be yours,
May peace and joy fill up your hours,
And may they glide as smooth away,
As sunbeams on a summer day ;
May never aught that brings distress,
Occur to mar your happiness,
Live so that death will bring no pain,
And die, that you may live again.

Give us Bread.*

Take physic, Pomp. Expose thyself to feel what wretches feel, that thou may'st shake the superflex to them, and show the Heavens more just.—*King Lear.*

DYING, dying in hundreds,
Starving for want of bread,
While thousands of acres remain untill'd,
From which millions might be fed.
O ! ye rulers of nations,
When will this misery cease—
When will the laws be made equal for all,
That the stores of the poor may increase ?

Have ye no bowels of mercy ?
Hardened and callous you've grown,
Till your hearts have been closed 'gainst the cries of the poor,
And when bread's asked you give them a stone.
Hark to their famishing groans !
Death takes its stand by their bed ;
Women and children and grey-haired sires
Are dying for want of bread.

Dying, dying in hundreds,
Starving with hunger and cold.
While nabobs drive fast by the homes of the poor,
" Shining in silver and gold."

*Written at the time of the bread riots in Exeter, England.

Riches and treasures in plenty
Are gathered in heaps through the land,
While Famine and Misery 's stalking abroad,
Like fiends going hand-in-hand.

When will the great and the wealthy
Be willing to share with the poor?
When will the artisan earn enough
To keep back the wolf from his door?
How long will the rich and the strong
Tread the poor man down in the dirt?
How long, oh God, how long
Must we sing " The Song of the Shirt?"

Where are You, John?

A few days ago, in a crowded court at the Assizes in Cobourg, a constable called aloud the somewhat familiar name of "John Smith," and received no answer. We question if such a thing could take place anywhere else in the civilized world.—*Hamilton Times.*

WHAT's become of all the "John Smiths"?
  Where's the "dear departed" gone?
Is it possible that Cobourg
  Never has been blessed with one?

Not a "Beak" in all the country
  (Barrin' Cobourg's) but will say
That there's some one of the family
  Up before him every day.

What is home without a mother-
  In-law for to quarrel with?
(One is just as bad's another,)
  What's a town without "John Smith?"

Nary one! Unhappy Cobourg,
  There is not another place
In the world that I have heard of
  Where John has not shewn his face.

Out where polygamy reigneth,
  Smiths are by the acre found,—
"Johns" and "Janes," as thick as locusts,
  Are encumbering the ground.

Would it not be well that Cobourg
    Should immediate action take,
And send an order out to Brigham
    To export some from Salt Lake?

In our other towns and cities
    They (the Smiths) have led the van
Till they have become more num'rous
    Than the famous Ku Klux Klan.

Smiths ! the Smiths are hydra headed ;
    Smiths grow up three deep in rows ;
Smiths, in countless hosts and legions,
    Everywhere have poked their nose.

Bummers, barristers and bakers,—
    Men not easily trifled with ;
Doctors, dyers, undertakers—
    Everybody's called John Smith.

Smithe the baliff, Smythe the barber,
    Schmidt that keeps the grocery store ;
Smith—by Jove ! there's Smith the tailor—
    Knocking at my chamber door,
Wanting me to *lend* him money,
    Only this and nothing more.

Smiths in every hole and corner,—
    Members both of church and state ;
Smiths in millions thro' this vast world
    Back and forward emigrate.

When one dies there are a dozen
   Ready to fill up his room ;
There's no doubt but what their line will
   Stretch unto " the crack of doom."

If the Smiths all left this planet,
   Any one can see quite plain,
It would cause so great a vacuum,
   Chaos would come back again.

On the map of our Dominion
   Cobourg will become a myth
If it can't support sev-er-al
   Families of the name of Smith.

Smith ! I'm out of breath ; the theme is
   Too great to descant upon.
Smith ! good gracious ! here's that tailor
   Coming back ; so good-bye, John.

Second Epistle to Wm. Murray, Esq.

My worthy friend and brother bard,
   King of Acrostics, prince of rhyme,
The laurels will be your reward,
   All your productions are sublime.

Green be your bays, and may they bloom
   And blossom yet for many years ;
May happiness reign in your home,
   Unmixed with sorrows, cares and tears.

May you and yours be blessed with all
   The joys which fortune has in store ;
May Heaven be open to your call.
   What honest man can wish you more ?

Reply to the Toast of the Press

At a Supper and Presentation given to J. W. HARRIS, Esq., *of the Hamilton* EVENING TIMES.

MR. CHAIRMAN and friends, I cannot do less,
Than say a few words to the toast of the Press;
At present, however, it's not my intention
To speak of the merits of that great invention;
Of its power to do good, or its power to do evil—
Though loved by the Angels 'tis leagued with a Devil;
And though it's a theme that your hearts may be fixed on,
It's been spoke for to-night by MCANDREW and NIXON.
So at present I think I will lay't on the shelf,
As the Press has a tongue that can speak for itself:
But this much I will say, it's pleasant to see
So many Press Printers sitting round about me,
Who have met here to-night with this object in view,
To give honour to one to whom honour is due;
And I honestly think that between here and Paris
Few more deserving are than Mr. JOHN HARRIS.
It is true he has faults, but they're faults of the head,
His heart with kind feelings is richly inlaid;
And you would not give him this token of merit
If virtue of some kind he did not inherit;
Long may he continue to gain your esteem,
Vice versa may you win the same thing from him;

While there's duty to do like " Barkiss " be willing,
May you ne'er be so poor that you'll see your last shilling ;
May your TIMES be good times, and may they extend
From Hamilton here to earth's uttermost end ;
Through storm and through sunshine, through foul and fair
    weather,
May the TIMES, he, and you all grow prosperous together ;
As your guest here to-night, let me wish you success,
May you prosper and flourish along with the Press.

The Spirit of the Times.

"The times are out of joint," all things seem changed,
Men now-a-days are turning quite deranged,
Morals and manners have been thrown aside,
Their places filled by Cant, Deceit and Pride;
Honor and Virtue are forgotten quite,
And Vice stalks forth a giant in his might;
Fraud and Corruption, like twin-brothers, meet
At every turn and corner of the street.

Men in "high places," holding rank and power,
Have fall'n beneath those evils of the hour,—
Placed in positions where they should be just,
Their lives are nothing but a " breach of trust."
Our " public men" have grown from bad to worse,
They sponge their living out the " public purse,"
Their minds seem filled with nothing else but gain,
The " silver question" 's rooted in their brain;
Unlike our merchants, they take it at par,
Grab all they can and then look out for more;
Brewers may cheat, or do just what they will,
As long's they send some "grist" unto their "mill."

Justice and Law are now as wide apart
As any rogue could wish them in his heart.
Law is a race-course where our lawyers run,
To see which side will have least justice done.

There's plenty Law, of Justice we're bereft—
At least there's very little of it left ;
Her sword is blunted, and her scales, of late,
Are seldom used, except to give " false weight,"
And as for " Truth," she stays within her well,
And " meek-eyed Mercy" 's gone with her to dwell ;
Plain " Common Sense" has vanished, God knows where,
And "Wisdom's seat" is made the " Scorner's chair."
Swindlers are plentier than they were before,
And P. T. Barnums flourish by the score.

Forgers and burglars drive a thriving trade,
To " jug" them now does not make them afraid ;
A few " loose hundreds" given from their " haul"
Will place a ladder on their prison wall,
Then if they choose they need not long remain,
But take " French leave" and " come the dodge " again.

Next unto them the gamblers take their rank,
Fleecing their victims nightly at the " bank,"
Winked at by those who ought to frown them down,
And banish them from every place around ;
Law-makers are law-breakers in their case,
For oft they are the " patrons" of their place ;
Thus screened from justice do they ply their trade,
And ruin thousands ere one fortune's made.
Madness and misery with their train all dwell
Within the precincts of a " gambling hell ;"
Yet are they carried on from day to day,
And none steps forward e'en to say them nay.

Eruptions in society are rife,
And " love your neighbor" means to " love his wife"—
Shew her around and with her cut a dash,
Ruin his peace and pocket all his cash ;
On " wings of love " you hasten then afar,
And hold your nuptials in a sleeping car.
Shattered and broken is the marriage vow,
And " easy virtue" is what's trumps just now.

Look at those " painted sepulchres" of sin,
Where fallen women hold their " court" within,
Just step inside and you will meet with them,
That *seem* respectable, but " are not what they seem ;"
Men who have families—aye, and honest wives
That stay at home and fret away their lives.
But who ne'er think their lords are bandying jests
With jades and wantons at those sweet " love feasts"—
She whom they swore to cherish and protect
Is left to pine in misery and neglect ;
Oh, would to Heaven that there could be some plan
To put a whip in every honest hand,
Expose these wretches—have their guilt unfurled—
And " lash the rascals naked through the world !"
It is indeed a curious age we live in,
When men who're trying to " win souls to Heaven"
Have been requested to resign their place*
For holding forth the means of " saving grace."

---

* It is stated as a fact, though we cannot vouch for its accuracy, that that good philanthropist Lord Cecil was requested by the Horse Guards to resign his commission.

Our soldiers need no saving grace at all,
They're " targets merely" just to stop a ball ;
The Horse Guards think (and they, of course, know best,)
Religion in a soldier is but jest.
They would not fight if they religious were,
And so they try to keep them as they are.
They say it would be to the nation's loss
If soldiers should be " Soldiers of the Cross,"
And beat their swords to ploughshares and give o'er
The trade of war and study it no more.

Let's hope the time is not far distant when
Society will be reformed again—
When knaves and roguery will be put to flight,
And be compelled to bid the world good-night,
When virtue will be lauded and extolled,
And prized more highly than the purest gold,
When all mankind in one great Brotherhood
Shall work together for each other's good.

On the late Stewart Malcomson, Esq.

THOU art gone to thy rest, all thy trials are o'er,
　And we would not recall thee again ;
Thy cross like a Christian you manfully bore
　Until death rent thy heartstrings in twain.

When the tidings which tell of thy death have been borne
　To thy birthplace, far over the sea,
A wail will rise up from the cliffs of Stromness—
　A wail of true sorrow for thee.

I'll not eulogize thee—our Maker alone
　Is entitled our actions to scan ;
But the coffin which covers thy ashes contains
　The remains of a true honest man.

A Vision.

I dreamt, and methought I was carried away
    On the wings of the wind to Heaven,
And I saw one there, 'mong the angels fair,
    Unto whom great joy was given.

A golden crown encircled his head,
    And his body was robed in white :
And he sat on a throne which brightly shone,
    And he gazed on a glorious sight.

For around him was gathered an angel band,
    With harps and psalteries strung,
And they all knelt down beside his throne,
    And they raised their voices and sung :

"Hail, brother, hail! we welcome thee
    To the land of the Great Divine,
And all the joys of Paradise
    Henceforward shall be thine ;

"For worthy art thou to reign with us,
    And share our joy always;
Then take this lyre, and join our choir,
    And sing to Jehovah's praise."

Then they led him away, but where they went
    I looked in vain to see ;
For the vision fled as I turned in my bed
    And awoke to reality.

John Smith.

"'Tis true, 'tis pity, and pity 'tis 'tis 'true.'—SHAKSPEARE.

JOHN SMITH was asked to subscribe, one day,
To a mission in Africa, far away.
"What is the mission for?" he said.
"To teach the heathen to write and read,
And explain the ways of Christian love
And the truths which lead to Heaven above."
"All right," quoth John.   From his pocket he drew
A cent and a dollar; he gave the two
To the man, who seemed to look rather strange,
And who asked what "he meant by a cent in change?"
"The cent's for the heathen," John Smith said,
"To increase the fund to teach them to read,
And become civilized, and to use the pen,
And cheat, and lie, like Christian men.
The dollar for *you* is most kindly meant;
You'll require the dollar to send out the cent.
You heathen at home are the worst of the two—
''Tis true, and a pity it is, 'tis true.'"
John wished him good-day and was soon out of sight.
But I cannot help thinking John Smith was right.

Women's Rights.

The editor of one of our exchanges says that the nine ladies who gave their votes at the late Presidential election, in Rochester, are deserving of a permanent place in history.

———

> Prepare for rhyme; I'll publish, right or wrong.
> Fools are my theme—let satire be my song.   BYRON.

———

THERE are nine wonders in the world,
  And each of them is a nine day's wonder ;
There are nine ladies in Rochester
  A greater wonder than them—by thunder.

They went to the polls to record their votes,
  And to claim their rights in legislation—
They thought that by mixing the sheep with the goats
  Would do much good to themselves and the nation.

To their minds the times seemed out of joint,
  And that women were suffering degradation ;
So they screwed their courage to the voting point,
  And tried to work out their own salvation.

" It takes nine tailors to make one man"—
  To say this seems to be making fun—
When these nine ladies, each in herself,
  Were equal to nine men made into one.

Ye nine who dwell on Parnassus' heights,
  When next ye sit down to drink your wine,
Don't fuddle away till you all get tight—
  But immortalize these ladies nine.

Give them a place in our history—
  Put Susan B. at the head of the line;
Set thou thy "mark" on this Antony—
  Cleopatra-like cause her to shine.

And you, ye poets of mickle fame.
  Who have drank deep draughts from Parnassian pools,
Cudgel your brains for a week or two,
  And eulogize these brainless fools.

I love one woman as dear as life—
  I try to respect all womankind—
But I hate these bearded and parded ones,
  With a high, Samsonic turn of mind.

I have heard of their doings oft enough,
  And the trouble they make, and fuss and pother;
Heaven has given to them one sphere,
  And they try to take to themselves another.

They jig, they amble, and gad about,
  And play fantastic tricks before
High Heaven, and then go home at night,
  To their "little beds," and lie down and snore.

I said they "snored"—I won't take it back;
  Whate'er men DARE they always DO.

In a few more moons I expect to hear
    That they smoke tobacco, and spit and chew.

They lie right down on their beds of down,
    And dream that men are but Fortune's fools;
Then they rise, with chignons on their crowns,
    And they try to push us from our stools.

A woman is lovely in her own sphere
    (Three yards in diameter, that's nine on the round,
With a train like the tail of a comet, in rear,
    Which daintily sweepeth all over the ground.)

Yes, woman is lovely in her own sphere;
    For bringing up babies she can't be beat,
Or running up bills in the dry goods line,
    She can knock the spots off a man complete.

I am tired of the capers which some of them cut,
    Their high-joint delusions and gaudy show;
As Hamlet said to his sweetheart once,
    " Let them go their ways—to a nunnery go."

But you, ye women of sense and worth,
    God's second best blessing unto man,
If you wish to retain your position on earth,
    Avoid these Amazons all that you can.

A woman is made for a man's helpmate—
    To make home happy and share his riches,
But not to go to the polls and vote,
    And come home *half slewed* in her husband's breeches.

The Grecian Bend.

THERE is a tide in the affairs of women
 Which differs slightly from the affairs of men ;
If taken at the flood it leads to fashion
 And fashion leads you to the Grecian Bend.

The Grecian Bend to something else leads on ;
 No matter what as long as it is strange.
Our women have like money-brokers grown ;
 They're always hunting after " Bills" and " change."

But shortly since they were all hooped like barrels,
 But now their skirts hang round them like a sack,
The *mode* is now for them to dress like camels,
 And wear a hump or two upon their back.

Poets have sung in tender strains and sweet,
 Of maidens tripping light as any fairy ;
But now our maidens limp along the street
 With " bunches " on them like a dromedary.

Fashion has played strange antics in her time,
 And silly goslings study in her school—
They should remember when she baits her line
 With flimsy gew-gaws, 'tis to catch a fool.

Much has been said and written of the chignon ;
 (I'm glad its reign is drawing to an end)
But give me, gods, a woman with a wig on
 Rather than one that has the Grecian Bend.

Canadian Women.

" THE proper study of mankind is man ;"
  But I think that he would be less than human
Who would not devote a part of his time
  To study man's counterpart—a woman.

If the tales are true that are told of her
  At the present time—or in bygone ages—
As wife, or mother, or widow, or maid,
  She's puzzled the brains of our wisest sages.

There are some, but they must be cynics, no doubt,
  Who don't keep their tongues fasten'd under hatches,
Declare that a woman is nothing more
  Than a thing made up out of shreds and patches.

Were they only judged by their flounces and frills,
  And the Fe-jee notions which Fashion bequeath them,
I grant you our cynics would then be right ;
  But they've warm, true hearts beating underneath them.

But what is mankind, I would like to know,
  But a piece of patch-work from the beginning ;
While women have been, as a general rule,
  Far oftener sinned against than sinning.

Poets have sung of their mothers-in-law,
  In many a strange and curious ditty ;

I'm not surprised at that, for the man
  Who (n)ever had one is an object of pity.

She is a friend that will stick to you close—
  Some men would say just as close as a blister;
Let those who wish to have comfort thro' life
  Get one, by marrying somebody's sister.

I've a wife myself, and I need not blush
  When I say that at present I'm very poor;
But I would not give this jewel of mine
  For a thousand rich gems like the Koh-i-noor.

We have our miffs and our tiffs, like the rest—
  Aye, as hot sometimes as a vapor bath—
But we always make it a steady rule
  That we ne'er let the sun go down on our wrath.

She is not an angel—at least, not quite—
  Tho' her bright eyes with love and kindness beam;
And I know myself I am not disposed
  To be gentle and mild like a cherubim.

I am only mortal—in this respect
  We are all alike, saints, sinners and seamen;
But there's no greater blessing on earth that I know,
  Than those lovely conundrums—Canadian women!

The Joys of Life Insurance.

An editor lives in the Buckeye State
  Who tries to do things for the best ;
He insured his life for a *very large sum*
  With some Companies way out West.

But he never once thought that by doing so
  He would often be forced to swear,
Nor did he believe that he'd ever become
  Such an object of special care.

He is wiser now.   If he's caught in a storm
  There are agents running round town
To protect him with lightning-rods, and they keep
  The lightning from knocking him down.

And in case he should manage to choke himself
  When he's asked by his friends to dine,
They are always on hand to wait upon him,
  And chop up his " hash " quite fine.

If he happens to walk by a river's brink,
  Or if e'er he goes in to swim,
They have life-preservers they carry along,
  And they throw four or five around him.

If he goes to shoot, he is followed then
  By the whole of the anxious staff,

And they always contrive to get him a gun
    That he can't persuade to go off.

If he goes for his "bitters" at early morn
    (Which editors do as a rule)
They will only allow him a three-inch horn,
    And that wont keep his coppers cool.

He is tired of life, and has told all his friends
    He would fain bid the world good bye !
But the Companies will not submit to this,
    And he can't get a chance to die.

We pity his fate ; it does seem very hard
    To be pestered like this thro' life ;
But we own that our sympathies are increased
    When *we think* of his *waiting* wife.

Poor woman ! her cares are a burden to her—
    She worrys and frets all the day,
And can take no comfort in saying her prayers
    Till he is got out of the way.

Impromptu

REPLY TO THE TOAST OF OUR GUESTS AT A SUPPER GIVEN BY
THE B. L. E. DIVISION NO. 133.

My Brothers, I'm glad to be with you all here,
Altho' I am not a Railway Engineer ;
Our connection for years has been drawn down so fine
Whate'er was your interest has also been mine ;
And I think that I am not committing a sin
When I claim to be one of your nearest of kin.
Be this my excuse for addressing you now,
Mr. Chairman, I make you my most polite bow.
It gives me great pleasure at present to mention
The success which attended your late great Convention,
And to know that your Order has done so much good,
Must be pleasing to all in this great Brotherhood.
The further and wider its influence extends
Has but helped to increase your large circle of friends ;
You must be well pleased when you know and you feel
There are many good men looking after your weal ;
'And there's few on this list, I am certain and sure,
Has your welfare at heart more than William K. Muir.
You also know well you need never ask twice
To find a good friend in *our* friend Joseph Price ;
And, last but not least, in fact, second to none,
Is our "Chief Engineer," W. A. Robinson.
But, you must not depend altogether on friends,

If you wish to attain any high worthy ends ;
In the world at large you must strive to do good,
Remember mankind is one vast Brotherhood.
And we do but our duty when we do all we can
To improve the condition of our fellow-man ;
There are no better mottoes to guide age or youth
Than your own one's—Sobriety, Justice and Truth—
Be true to yourselves—let your ambition be
To found more Divisions like One Thirty-Three.
May you all take delight in the good work begun,
And try to retain the position you've won.
Your path, then, right onward and upward will be,
As resistless as Sherman's great " March to the Sea."
Excuse my poor speech, it is bad at the best,
But I thank you all here, as becometh your guest.

The Wood Question.

SPOKEN AT ST. JAMES' HALL, HAMILTON, AT A RE-UNION FOR THE
PURPOSE OF GETTING WOOD FOR THE POOR.

ROGUERY there is in all trades—that is partly understood ;
But there's nothing else than roguery nowadays, in selling
   wood.
Greedy vampires fill our market—men whose consciences
   are gone.
Or if they have any left yet, it has been turn'd into stone.

There may be some few exceptions, but they're very seldom
   seen ;
Most of them will try to fleece you if they find that you are
   green.
Every time they bring a load in, charge you higher than
   before—
Like the paupers with the pea-soup, still keep bawling out
   for more.

Only think of what they charge you ! is it really not absurd,
That we must pay Seven Dollars, sometimes, for a single
   cord ?
There are many in the city who could scarcely buy't before,
Now it is out of their power entirely for to purchase any
   more.

See yon poor, half-famished widow—tears are stealing down
  her cheek—
Shivering in her scanty garments, scarcely able e'en to speak ;
Having toiled and scraped together all the money that she
  could,
Pleads as if she plead for mercy to obtain a load of wood !

See the burly wretch beside her crack his whip and turn
  away,—
" Mistress, you can have no wood here from us at that price
  to-day."
Vain her wailing !—vain her pleading !—back again she
  must retire
To her little famished household, where there's neither food
  nor fire.

Think of this, you that have money—think of what the
  honest poor,
Through the biting days of winter, in their misery must
  endure ;
Think of those whose scanty wages scarce suffice to purchase
  food,
Then you'll come to learn the value there is in a cord of
  wood,

Canada's Appeal to the "Paris" Crew.*

LAY to your oars, my hearts of oak,
    And do your duty now,
For England means to pluck away
    The laurels from your brow.
Our hopes are centred in your powers,
    Then deftly ply the oar,
And try to place your country's flag
    In triumph at the fore.
Then ply your oars, my hearts of oak,
    And give way with a will ;
A long, a strong and steady stroke
    Will keep you Champions still.

Newcastle glories in her sons,
    And vaunts her dauntless crew ;
Show them that Canada can boast
    Of gallant oarsmen too—
Men who have ne'er defeated been
    In any race they've run,
And who, we hope, will still retain
    The honors they have won.
Then ply your oars, my hearts of oak,
    And give way with a will ;

A long, a strong and steady stroke
    Will keep you Champions still.

Vict'ry has often times before
    Been seated on your prow—
Deserve success and she will not
    Forsake or leave you now ;
Your country's honor's in your hand,
    Your laurels still are green,
And may another triumph yet
    Await you at Lachine.
Then ply your oars, my hearts of oak,
    And give way with a will ;
A long, a strong and steady stroke
    Will keep you Champions still.

The Printer.

Alas ! poor Yorick, I knew him well, Horatio.—Shakspeare,

THE Printer leads a happy life—
  He works both night and day,
And spends his hours in usefulness
  While others sleep or play ;
As cheerful as a galley slave
  He toils his life away.

His pockets always are well lined
  With " nothing much" inside,
And as he's not a millionaire,
  He has not any pride ;
He needs but little here below,
  And little's not denied.

From sunny morn till dewy eve
  He jogs along his way,
Rebuffs he takes for compliments,
  And almost *nix* for pay—
He seems a sort of " happy cuss"
  On whom the people prey.

To love his neighbor as himself
  Has always been his plan,
And when he's socially inclined
  He goes to " see a man,"

And, in a philanthropic way,
    Shakes " Old Tom " by the hand.

When age creeps on him, and he finds
    His brows with furrows bent,
He meets with sympathizing friends
    Who do not care a cent
In what way his existence ends,
    Or howsoe'er 'twas spent.

His life he gives for other's good,
    And though it might seem funny,
He lives on bitters all his days
    Instead of milk and honey,
And dies beloved by every man
    Who ever owed him money.

To get his life insured, in life
    He very often tried,
But as he couldn't raise the stamps,
    He ne'er was gratified ;
His epitaph was written thus :
    " He lived, and moved, and—died."

Delays are Dangerous.

DELAYS are dangerous things, and oft
　　Bring trouble in their train ;
One moment lose, and you can ne'er
　　Recall it back again ;
Then whatsoe'er you have to do,
　　Don't linger by the way,
Or else you'll find the proverb true,
　　There's danger in delay.

Shakspeare has said there is a tide
　　In the affairs of men
That must be taken at the flood
　　If you would fortune gain ;
But if the chance you seize not then,
　　'Twill ebb and flow away,
And seldom e'er returns again—
　　Then trust not to delay.

The present moment's all we have
　　That we can call our own :
We know not what nor where we'll be
　　Before the day is done ;
Then while the sun is shining bright,
　　Be sure you make your hay,
And go to work with all your might—
　　There's danger in delay.

Procrastination is a thief,
 And him we all should dread :
He steals the time away by which
 We earn our daily bread ;
If you should meet him on the road,
 Pass on another way,
Don't take him back to your abode,
 There's danger in delay.

But take time by the forelock if
 You want to gain success,
For on this, to a great extent,
 Depends your happiness.
Don't let until to-morrow stand
 What can be done to-day ;
Do what you have to do off-hand,
 And never trust delay.

Glackmeyer's Soliloquy

(AFTER PRINCE ARTHUR HAD VISITED LONDON.)

THE Prince has gone, and I am glad he has ;
   I wish to Heaven that he ne'er had come ;
Confusion now hath made its masterpiece
Of ev'rything that is around my home.

My halls have been made desolate, and all
   My Brussels carpets trampled on and torn—
Or, what's as bad, been spattered o'er with suds.
   Oh ! would to Heaven he had ne'er been born.

The Lord's anointed temple has been robbed—
   At least my cellar has, of all its beer,
By guards of honor—honor in a horn !
   Where is the honor in a Volunteer ?

Hooked are my grapes—four hundred pounds or more;
   My trees and vines have all been broken down ;
No wonder is it that I feel so sore—
   That I by them should have been done so brown.

May furies seize the wretch that took away
   My sister's stockings and my pantaloons ;
Accursed be the ground he treads to-day—
   A wonder 'tis he did not take my spoons.

Two warlike steeds within my stables stood
  Devouring oats and gormandizing hay;
Three days I fed them on the best of food,
  And now the scrubs refuse for them to pay.

But I will have revenge—revenge is sweet;
  And I will make them dearly rue the day
They ever set their feet within my house;
  They'll find they'll have the very devil to pay.

What care I though the people say I'm mean;
  They can't say aught that I myself don't know;
I can't afford to play the host for them
  Whene'er they choose to have a raree-show.

Unhappy's he who on a Prince doth wait,
  But he who waits upon their *suite* does worse;
A fig for loyalty! Glackmeyer the Great
  Waited to put some "money in his purse."

Canada to Brother Jonathan.

O JONATHAN my jo, Jon,
    I wonder what you mean
By raisin' sic a fuss, Jon—
    The like was never seen ;
You'll hae the hale o' Europe, Jon,
    Upon you ere ye know,
Then you'll need to haul your horns in,
    Dear Jonathan my jo.

O Jonathan my jo, Jon,
    To me it's very plain
You want to get fair Cuba's isle
    Awa frae bonnie Spain ;
But gin ye try to tak' it, Jon,
    John Bull and wee Crapeau
Will gar ye wish ye'd stayed at hame,
    Dear Jonathan my jo.

O Jonathan my jo, Jon,
    You arena very blate—
I'm tauld you're wantin' Canada,
    To mak' a braw new State—
But ye can tak' my word, Jon,
    Wi' you we ne'er will go,
As long as we respect oursel's,
    Dear Jonathan my jo.

O Jonathan my jo, Jon,
  (I dinna say't in scorn)
But whiles I think you're unco fond
  O "tootin'" on your horn;
You've aye a lot of bounce, Jon,
  An' bluff, and brag, and blow,
But you've wasted muckle wind for nocht,
  Dear Jonathan my jo.

Then Jonathan my jo, Jon,
  Tak' this advice frae me:
When dogs are lyin' quiet and still,
  It's best to let them be—
For gin they're waukened up, Jon,
  Their teeth they're apt to show,
An' you'll find *their bite waur than their bark*,
  Dear Jonathan my jo.

O Jonathan my jo, Jon,
  We'd like to be your friends,
But this, unto a great extent,
  Upon yoursel' depends;
If you'll do what is richt, Jon,
  Then hand-in-hand we'll go,
And we'll lo'e ye yet for auld lang syne,
  Dear Jonathan my jo.

A Tale of the City.

ONE evening when the stars were shining,
  Brightly in the deep blue sky,
Laura stood beside her lover,
  Where a brook ran murmuring by.

'Neath a tree whose leafy branches
  Shaded them from human sight,
William pledged his troth eternal—
  Vowed he'd love her from that night.

Long and earnestly he pleaded
  That she would become his bride,
Telling her he fondly prized her
  More than all the world beside.

And he said if he should ever
  Lightly hold the marriage vows,
· She might use her best endeavor
  To procure another spouse.

Laura, who was unsuspicious,
  (Maidens ever are, in sooth,)
Listened to his words with pleasure,
  Thinking they were Gospel truth.

Then she gave her hand to William,
  Swore she'd always true remain,

William pressed her to his bosom,
   Kissed her o'er and o'er again.

Next morn he got the marriage license,
   That same day the knot was tied,
William was a joyous bridegroom,
   Laura was a happy bride.

But joy, alas ! won't last forever,
   Our path through life is sometimes thorny,
William passed the night in clover,
   And "cleared" next day for "Californy."

Laura cried at his departure,
   But her grief she soon did smother,
And before the week was over,
   She "levanted" with another,

Our Gallant "Fire Brigade."

ALL honor to our "Fire Brigade,"
   The gallant and the brave ;
"Aye ready !" are they in our need —
   They always "run to save."
By night or day they ne'er refuse
   To lend their willing aid,
But do their duty manfully—
   Our gallant "Fire Brigade."

No coward fears their hearts assail ;
   Their nerves are strong as steel,
And often do they risk their lives
   For sake of others' weal.
Tho' danger stares them in the face
   They never are afraid,
But strike the lions from their path—
   Our gallant " Fire Brigade !"

Whene'er the " dread alarm" is raised
   No time by them is lost ;
They hurry forward to the fire,
   Each man is at his post.
And fierce the fiery flames must be
   Whose progress can't be stayed
When they're opposed by men like these
   Who form our "Fire Brigade."

Whence come those agonizing screams
   .   At intervals between?
Look! at yon window, thro' the smoke,
   A living form is seen!
" Hooks! raise your ladders to the top,
   Quick!—quick, boys!—lend your aid!"
Up, up they mount! She's saved—she's saved!
   God bless our " Fire Brigade!"

'Tis these, and daring deeds like these,
   Which make our Firemen loved ;
In many a hard and trying scene
   Their courage has been proved.
Green be the bays they've won, and may
   Their laurels never fade !
And may success still wait upon
   Our gallant " Fire Brigade!"

Beautiful Snow.

"Now the 'Evens bless the Pollis Court and all its bold ver-dicts."—THACKERAY.

BEAUTIFUL snow !   Beautiful snow !
What a pity it is that you bother us so ;
In the country 'tis gladness to see you come down,
But 'tis different quite when you fall in the town.
If you lie on our sidewalks an inch thick or so,
Then we're hauled up and fined for not shov'lling the snow.

Sensible laws !   Sensible laws !
By which we are fined when there's not any cause.
Our Magistrate sits like a king on his throne,
Dispensing a code that's entirely his own ;
What a mockery of justice they are, we all know,
Especially this one with regard to the snow.

Beautiful town !   Beautiful town !
Where our Mayor and Aldermen often sit down
To discuss what is best for the " public weal,"
O'er a dish of mock turtle (at Lee's) or green seal ;
But I cannot conceive how they could blunder so,
As to draft such a silly by-law about snow.

Alderman Kelly !   Alderman Kelly !
May the whale that had Jonah three days in its belly
Be stuffed with the members of our Corporation,
If they don't try and bring about some reformation.

I don't include you—you're straightforward, I know,
And said what was right on this question of snow.

    Dutiful peelers !   Dutiful peelers !
Whose business it is to watch " pickers and stealers ;"
To quell lawless riot and keep crime in check,
Is the duty of both the police and the " beak."
But don't let the thieves and the burglars all go,
And make a great haul out a " wee pickle " snow.

    Brotherly love !   Brotherly love !
My spirit with kindness and pity you move.
I am glad I have learned to return good for evil,
Or I'd wish the whole batch of them were at—the dévil,
Or in some shady spot where no warm breezes blow,
Buried five fathoms deep 'neath the beautiful snow.

Wanted.

MR. EDITOR,
   SIR,—
I've been reading your paper,
(I'm the person that sent you the new pair of pants),
And of course you'll allow me the use of your columns :
I want to discourse on your chapter of " wants."

To begin with, I notice a number of " wanters :"
Some want to rent houses—some houses to let ;
But of one thing I'm sure, there are great numbers wanting
A great many things that they never will get.

Wanted three-score cabinetmakers, et cetera,
To work in the factory on Bay street and York ;
Wanted a housemaid by Mrs. G., Duke street,
Wanted a man that knows how to pack pork.

Wanted a dozen good general servants.
Good general servants ! there is no such thing ;
Our servants (more pity) have all turned our masters—
Whenever they choose it they give us the fling.

Wanted a cook—the Lord sends us victuals,
The devil sends cooks (so I've heard sailors say) ;
Too many cooks spoil the broth—that we never
May want any cooks in *our* house, let us pray.

Wanted a boy to be active and *useful*—
  As well might you ask for the man in the moon
To stand in the Square on some Saturday evening
  Beside the new bell-tower, and whistle a tune.

Wanted a nurse that has got *some* experience—
  That's a libel on nurses,—whoever saw one,
That had not got experience enough for a dozen?
  There is nothing new to them under the sun.

A gentleman wants a good bedroom with *board;*
  It is lucky for him he don't want any more;
Any person who has such a thing at disposal,
  Will please address ALFRED, box one-forty-four.

Wanted one tailor and two tailoresses;
  Wanted a milliner—aye, there's the rub;
That's the calamity makes life a burden,
  Our millinery costs twice as much as our grub,

Two or three joiners and carpenters wanted;
  They must all be good hands and none of them green;
Wanted ten pant-makers, Sintzel & Bartman;
  Two men to press cloth with a pressing machine.

Wanted a stout, active boy at the straw works,
  He's wanted to work, not to study the law;
There's plenty of these in our city already—
  Beside this our lawyers are not "men of straw."

Wanted a teamster, one steady and sober,
  He must write a fair hand, and not get on the spree;

Good references wanted (in a horn!—that's all bunkum)
  Apply at the office of the Spring Brewery.

A widow is wanting a good situation;
  (God help all the widows !) I hope she'll get one ;
Jordan, to them, is a hard road to travel,
  Thorns grow on the pathway o'er which they must run.

Wanted a railway to go the to north-west,   *
  (There's a fine chance for some one to grind a big axe ;)
Wanted a bonus—a cool hundred thousand,—
  Lord grant us the money to pay for this tax !

Wanted, the world and his wife, for their profit,
  To advertise in and subscribe for the TIMES ;
Wanted a poet more *pun*-gent than Wingfield,
  WANTED—

(We decline to insert any more of these rhymes.—ED.)

Bob Berry,

Winner of the 3-mile single-scull race, at the Buffalo Regatta, held on the 4th of July, 1872.

CANADIANS, your glasses fill up to the brim,
To night let us all be quite merry,
And drink to that famed dusky oarsman so trim—
Our Canadian Champion, Bob Berry.

At Buffalo our honor he nobly sustained,
Tho' Fortune at first was contrary;
When the race was repeated, the victory was gained
By the great Prince of Scullers, Bob Berry.

Bob, Bob, Bob, Bob !
By that great Prince of Scullers, Bob Berry.

His opponent was Coulter, who oftentimes bragged
He could whip all the rest of creation ;
But Bob quickly caused him to haul down his flag.
In sight of the great Yankee nation !

While we honor Bob's name, let us drink to his fame
In a bumper of champagne or sherry ;
The laurels he won may he stoutly maintain—
Hip, hurrah ! here's a health to Bob Berry !

Bob, Bob, Bob, Bob !
Our Canadian Champion, Bob Berry !

Miscellaneous.

Going One Better.

"A great man's memory may outlive his life for half a year; but, by Our Lady, he'll have to build churches then."—HAMLET.

A WOMAN in town, who got " spliced" to John Robb,
  (A turner of wood and a maker of bobbins),
Was well pleased with her lord until death cut his stick,
  Then she went and got wed to another—called Robbins.

For a while they were happy as bugs in a rug;
  But he, too, " pegged out," and this ended their fun.
Few—few—were the tears that she shed on his bier,
  Then she married a friend of his named Robinson.

They "billed" and they "cooed" for the space of a year,
  (Of happier couples there were very few so),
He died, like the others, and she's casting sheep's eyes
  At a lineal descendant of Robinson Crusoe.

Meteorological.

" GLOOMY winter's noo awa',"
  At least 'twas thocht sae by us a';
But feth we hae been sair mista'en,
For gloomy winter's come again,

An' blawin' fiercely up the lake,
The cauld east wind aft gars us shake.
March cam' in Lion-like, wi' vigour,
An' gangs oot wi' uncommon rigour,
Sweet April (bashful maiden), she
Stan's wi' the tear-drap in her e'e,
Afeard to come and laith to stay,
Till urged on by her sister May,
 She dights her e'en an' sings a sang,
An' smiling gently comes alang.

Breezy.

A POET by the name of Breeze,
Whose writings are considered terse,
Is trying now to raise the wind
By getting up a blast of verse—
'Tis said there's plenty of it too,
And that his strains are sure to please us :
They're " windy," but that's nothing new,
One breeze keeps blowing other breezes.

A Child's Thought.

'TWAS a beautiful thought of a little girl,
 Who stood, at the evening's close,
And looked at three tiny buds peeping out
 On a branch by a faded rose :

"Come, Willie, and see those sweet little buds,"
    The child to her brother cries ;
"They have waken'd up just in time to kiss
    Their mother before she dies."

Impromptu Apostrophe to Rosa D'Erina

(Whilst listening to the artiste's beautiful rendition of "Kathleen,
    Mavourneen," and other Irish melodies.)

HAIL to thee, matchless Queen of Song,
    Worthy the mantle of fam'd Catharine Hayes ;
Thy memory will be cherished long
    By those who've listened to thy glorious lays.
Thy country's genius is enthron'd in thee,
    Exponent of the Green Isle's minstrelsy.

Impromptu

(While looking at the arch at Alderman Glackmeyer's residence in
    London, erected in honor of Prince Arthur.)

"TAKE down that arch, thou greedy scrub,
    And when the Prince next visits here,
Don't charge him quite so much for grub ;
    Be honest if you're not sincere."

Poets' Names.

What poet is the tallest one ?
    Longfellow is his name,
Who worked in precious metals ?
    Goldsmith of village fame.

Who realized the use of words?
Why *Wordsworth*, to be sure.
Key was permitted to unlock
The muse's escruitor.

And which one was a sufferer?
Paine suffered very keen ;
White could not be a colored man ;
There's " verdancy " in *Green.*

Who rung the changes now and then ?
Campbell, who sung of " Hope,"
And what one was infallible?
That grand old satirist *Pope.*

And who had the most warlike name
Of any one that's here?
He who was greater than them all—
The world's Bard, *Shakspeare.*

———————◆———————

Which author wrote most ?—Bulwer, Warren or Dickens?
It is certain they all made great use of the pen.
Bulwer's friends all maintain that he wrote " Night and
Morning ;"
While Warren, 'tis said, only wrote " Now and Then ;"
But Dickens, than either, wrote more, I'll be bound,
For 'tis very well known he wrote " All the Year Round."

Marriage Notices.

(On the Marriage of Mr. Joshua Filman to Miss Emma Matilda
   Sovereign, East Flamboro', Feb. 12th, 1873.)

FILMAN, my boy, I give you joy
   In getting such a wife ;
While you have her you'll never want
   A sovereign in your life.

A virtuous woman is worth gold—
   With gold you can't be poor ;
Your sovereign—in your case—will make
   Assurance doubly sure.

May she be versed in wisdom's ways,
   And never turn a shrew ;
Nor prove her right to sovereignty
   By ruling over you.

Love one another all you can ;
   By Hymen still be led ;
And may your path throughout this life
   With sovereign gifts be spread.

(Mr. T. Winkle to Miss Rachael Starr.)

" MARRIAGES are made in Heaven,"
(Our happiness they make or mar ;)

T. Winkle chose this mode of living,
　To get " hitched" to Rachael Starr.
In the summer, in the autumn,
　In the winter, in the spring,
May she shed refulgence round him,
　While he keeps a Twinkle-ing.

———————

(The poet, Carroll Ryan, of the Ottawa *Evening Mail*, has married
　Miss McIvor, a poetess, also of Ottawa.)

No DOUBT the little Ryans will
　Be taught to carol very sweetly ;
As both the parent birds can sing,
　They'll fill the house with song completely.

God bless the poet and his mate,
　Who have been bound in Hymen's tether,
And may the warblers long be spared
　To sing their Madrigals together.

———————

(On the Marriage of Mr. George Wright to Miss Olive Newell Wrong,
　by the Rev. J. Schulte, rector of Port Burwell.)

LET Burwell's citizens rejoice,
　And let them all unite
In blessing Schulte, for he is one
　Who turns Wrong into Wright.
Thrice blessed be the happy pair,
　And may they find delight
In married life, and soon bring forth
　A little *wee* " All-Right."

(At West Flamboro', Miss Emma Wheat to Mr. Richard Bickle.)

Miss WHEAT got ripe for Cupid's joys,
   And then she fell 'neath Hymen's sickle ;
I hope her path may flowery be,
   And ne'er be thrashed by Richard Bickle.

Poetical Addresses on Letters.

" WHERE the sweet-scented coal oil spreads perfume around,
In the city of London, resides Thomas Browne;
Where, for fifteen years past, he has made his abode,
Near to Adelaide street, on the Hamilton road.
Not rich, yet not poor, one of earth's honest toilers,
A maker of oil stills and all kinds of boilers ;
This paper's for him, and I may as well state
His post office box is ' E '—*one twenty-eight.*"

To THE Senate at Ottawa this letter send ;
To the Acting Postmaster, Jas. Wingfield, my friend.
There is no stamp upon it, there's none needs to be,
For letters addressed unto Jamie gang free.

To ADAM BROWN, of Hamilton,
   This letter must be given ;
You'll find his store upon the Gore,
   It's number six from seven.
His office there is up one stair,
   Just twelve feet nearer Heaven,
Where those who deal for cash will find
   The best of bargains given.

POSTMAN, take heed, this letter speed
   Pacific-ward upon its journey
To William Onyon, Natonia street,
   In San Francisco, Californy,
That moral, virtuous, pious town
   Where Laura Fair goes "bobbin' round."

SONGS.

Fair Canada. *

LET others sing of sunny climes—
   Of lands beyond the sea ;
There's not a dearer spot on earth
   Than Canada to me.
      Dear Canada, loved Canada ;
         Wherever I may be,
      There's not a land on all the earth
         Shall win my heart from thee.

Her sons will ne'er submit to crouch
   Beneath a tyrant's sway ;
The stag that roams her forest glades
   Is not more free than they.
      Dear Canada, loved Canada ;
         Wherever I may be,
      There's not a land on all the earth
         Shall win my heart from thee.

The red-cross flag our fathers raised,
   We hail it as a friend,

---

* Set to music by G. F. DeVine.

And should that flag e'er be assailed,
　It's glories we'll defend.
　　　Fair Canada, brave Canada,
　　　　No land on earth more free ;
　　　And his would be a coward's arm
　　　　That would not strike for thee,

The Scot may boast his heather hills,
　The Englishman his rose,
And Erin's sons may love the vales
　Where Erin's shamrock grows. .
　　　But Canada, loved Canada,
　　　　Is dearer far to me ;
　　　No other land, however grand,
　　　　Shall win my heart from thee.

The sun that tints her maple trees
　With Nature's magic wand,
Shines down on peaceful, happy homes,
　In our Canadian land.
　　　Fair Canada, loved Canada,
　　　　My heart is wed to thee ;
　　　Be thou the land of noble deeds,
　　　　And Empire of the free.

The Lovely Maid of Hamilton.

THE maids of Canada are fair,
  And bear the palm where'er they go,
And loveliest of the maidens there
  Are found within Ontario.
But if you ask me where to find
  The sweetest, dearest, fairest one—
The paragon of womankind—
  Her dwelling place is Hamilton.
      The lovely maid of Hamilton,
      The charming maid of Hamilton ;
      Young Alice Dean is beauty's queen,
      And reigns supreme in Hamilton.

Grace sits enthroned upon her brow,
  And rosy health blooms in her cheeks,
Her voice is sweet, and soft, and low,
  And sounds like music when she speaks.
The lilies of the field are fair
  And beautiful to look upon,
But fairer than the lilies are,
  Is Alice Dean of Hamilton.
      The lovely maid of Hamilton,
      The charming maid of Hamilton ;
      Young Alice Dean is beauty's queen,
      And reigns supreme in Hamilton.

Her heart untainted is by guile—
  From pride and vanity she's free ;
A perfect heaven is in her smile,
  Her eye beams bright with modesty ;
Her's is a pure unsullied mind—
  If earth has angels she is one,
For all the graces are combined
  In Alice Dean of Hamilton.
        The lovely maid of Hamilton,
        The charming maid of Hamilton ;
        Young Alice Dean is beauty's queen,
        And reigns supreme in Hamilton,

The Wee Pet Lammie.

AIR—"*Annie Laurie.*"

I HAE a wee pet lammie—
  O' simmers she's seen three,
The picture o' her mammie,
  An' she's unco dear to me.
She is unco dear to me,
  She's a blythe wee cuddlin' doo,
An' the humming-bird wi' pleasure
  Micht pree her rosy mou'.

Like laverocks when they're singin'
  Up in the lift sae blue,
Her merry voice is ringin'
  Wi' joy the hale day thro'.
Wi' joy the hale day thro',
  She fills the house wi' glee;
An' the wee, wee laughin' fairy
  Is a treasure aye to me.

She rins aboot the yardie,
  An' pu's the bits o' flow'rs
As happy as a birdie
  Amang the simmer bow'rs.
Amang the simmer bow'rs,
  When blossoms deck ilk tree;

But there's ne'er a flow'r amang them
   That fairer is than she.

Her hair's like gowden nettin',
   When wavin' in the win';
A gem o' nature's settin'
   Is the dimple on her chin.
Is the dimple on her chin,
   She's the apple o' my e'e,
An' whate'er she is to ithers,
   She's a warld o' joy to me.

Athol's Bonnie Gem.

AIR—"*Morag's Faery Glen.*"

On Athol Bank the flowers bloom gay,
 And fresh and bright and fair;
But PHILLIS is the sweetest flower
 That sheds its blossom there.
The "modest daisy, crimson-tipp'd,"
 When morning opes its e'e,
Looks round on nothing half so sweet
 Nor half so fair as she.

And oh! may Heaven shield that flower,
 And guard its parent stem,
And all its choicest blessings shower
 On Athol's Bonnie Gem.

The robin trills its sweetest song,
 When PHILLIS passes by;
The rose with envy droops its head
 When PHILLIS cometh nigh;
And Phœbus shines on Athol Bank
 And tints the flow'rets fair;
But PHILLIS is the sweetest flower
 That buds and blossoms there.

And oh! may Heaven shield that flower,
 And guard its parent stem,
And all its choicest blessings shower
 On Athol's Bonnie Gem.

I'll Aye be True to Thee.

Young Maggie was the fairest lass
    In a' our bonnie toon,
And lang I wooed her for my bride,
    Ere her consent I won.
But weel I mind ae summer nicht,
    When Maggie said to me—
" Hae here's my hand, my heart's your ain,
    " I'll aye be true to thee."

Her hinnyed words fell on my ear
    As soft as maiden's prayer ;
I clasped her to my heart and vowed
    To love her evermair.
She blushed awhile and hung her head,
    And whispering, said to me—
" Ye've lov'd me lang, I've proved ye weel :
    " And I'll be true to thee."

But mony years hae passed since then,
    And years o' bliss they've been ;
The rose still blooms upon her cheek,
    And love lights up her een ;
And mem'ry aye brings back the nicht
    When Maggie said to me—
" Hae here's my hand, my heart's your ain,
    " I'll aye be true to thee."

I Dinna Ken.

AIR—"*There's nae room for twa.*"

'TWAS just about the gloamin' hour
    When Jeanie gaed awa'
Across the fields to meet wi' ane
    She lo'ed the best of a'.
The trysting tree soon cam' in view,
    And there stood Willie Glen,
Wha asked if "he might pree her mou'."
    Quo' she, "I dinna ken;
      I dinna ken ava," quo' she,
      "I dinna ken ava;
      Ye're sic a deil, when ye get ane
      That ye'll be wanting twa."

Now, Willie he had lo'ed her lang
    Wi' heart baith leal and true;
He kissed her lips sae saft and sweet,
    And praised her e'en o' blue;
Then speird when she would mak' o' him
    The happiest o' men?
Young Jeanie placed her han' in his
    And said "I dinna ken;
      I dinna ken ava," quo' she,
      "I dinna ken ava;
      I dout ye'll hae to wait for me
      Anither year or twa.

" Ye ken my faither's auld and frail ;
My mither's deid and gane ;
I couldna hae the heart to lea'
The puir auld man alane."
" But, Jeanie, lass, he'll aye find room
Within our ' but and ben.' "
Sin' that's the case, hae here's my han',
And mak' me Jeanie Glen ;
And mak' me Jeanie Glen," quo' she,
" And mak' me Jeanie Glen ;
I'll say nae mair, my Willie, dear,
I dinna, dinna ken."

Dan Black.

(Sung at a Festival of the Amalgamated Society of Engineers.)

YE'LL a' hae heard tell o' Dan Black, Dan Black ;
He's a man that's liked well is Dan Black, Dan Black ;
  He's an auld fashioned chiel
  That's as pawkie's the deil,
An' a heart true as steel has Dan Black, Dan Black.

He keeps a bit house on James Street, does Dan Black,
Where the " Western Boys " aften meet wi' Dan Black ;
  Ye may gang a' aroun'
  Frae saloon to saloon,
But the best hoose in toon is Dan Black's, Dan Black's.

If ye happen to stap in at nicht to Dan Black's
Ye'll see naething there but what's richt at Dan Black's ;
  He's aff-handed an' clean
  When he meets wi' a frien',
An' there's naething that's mean in Dan Black, Dan Black.

He's fond o' a crack an' a joke, is Dan Black ;
He likes a guid lauch an' a smoke, does Dan Black ;
  He's crouse an' he's cantie,
  He's bauld an' he's vauntie,
An' game as a bantie, Dan Black, Dan Black.

He's a wonderfu' bodie, Dan Black, Dan Black ;
He's as strong as a cuddie, Dan Black, Dan Black ;
    Tho' his stature's but sma',
    He's a match maist for twa,
If ye happen to thraw wi' Dan Black, Dan Black.

There's no muckle stuff left to spare in Dan Black
Yet it's a' geyin guid what is there o' Dan Black ;
    He's blythe an' he's free
    When he's aff on a spree,
Wi' his hat cock'd ajee, is Dan Black, Dan Black.

Here's wishin' you every success, Dan Black,
May your shadow, tho' sma', ne'er grow less, Dan Black,
    An' when years hae gane by,
    An' ye're laid out to dry,
May we a' meet on high wi' Dan Black, Dan Black.

A Wifie o' Your Ain.

COME, a' ye crusty bachelors, that lead a dreary life,
Get rid o' a' your miseries and tak' yoursel's a wife,
For you'll fin' an unco difference, by lying a' your lane,
When you come to ken the comforts o' a wifie o' your ain.
　　　　　A wifie o' your ain, O,
　　　　　A wifie o' your ain,
When you come to ken the comforts o' a wifie o' your ain.

At nicht when ye come hame frae wark, what pleasure is't
　　to see
The love-blinks that are dancin' aye within your wifie's e'e,
While she looks pleased and happy, and as proud as ony
　　queen,
It mak's you glad to think you ha'e a wifie o' your ain.
　　　　　A wifie o' your ain, O,
　　　　　A wifie o' your ain ;
It mak's you glad to think you ha'e a wifie o' your ain.

When man cam' on the earth at first his pleasures were but
　　sma',
Indeed it might be said that life had got nae charms ava,
Till he wauken'd up ae mornin' and it made him unco fain
To fin' close lyin' by his side a wifie o' his ain.
　　　　　A wifie o' his ain, O
　　　　　A wifie o' his ain ;
Man ne'er was blest till ance he found a wifie o' his ain.

Noo, ilka ane that lo'es his wife will prize her virtues high ;
For me I dinna wonder that he lauds her to the sky.
Ilk ane thinks aye their ain the best, and that's just sae wi'
    me,
For I wudna gi'e my ain guid wife for a' the wives I see.
        No, for a' the wives I see,
        No, for a' the wives I see,
I wudna gi'e my ain wee wife for a' the wives I see.

Johnnie Waugh.*

AIR—"*Laird o' Cockpen.*"

AN auld farrant bodie is wee Johnnie Waugh;
A kenspeckle bodie is auld Johnnie Waugh;
There's no muckle o' him—in stature he's sma'—
But he's warsled thro' life for three-score years an' twa.

He's hale an' he's hearty, he's blythe an' he's free,
An' for an auld man he's as brisk as a bee;
To Kirk upon Sunday he gangs aye fu' braw—
There's nane mair respecket than auld Johnnie Waugh.

If things whiles gang gleyd or a wee bit ajee,
Johnnie just gies a lauch, says, "Its a' ane to me."
He cares na a preen for the great nor the sma'—
Straughtforward an' honest is auld Johnnie Waugh.

Tho' his form's a wee bent an' his locks hae turned white,
In guid, social freen'ship he still tak's delight;
He believes that "mankind should be brethren a';"
The king o' guid fellows is auld Johnnie Waugh.

His wifie an' he are as cantie an' couth
As they were when at first they foregathered in youth.

---

* A "Scots worthy," an old and respected resident of Hamilton, and one of the original founders of the Central Presbyterian Church of that city.

Ye may search the hale kintra—ye winna find twa
Mair loving than Mary an' auld Johnnie Waugh.

May peace in their dwellin' continue to reign ;
Lang may they be spared amang freen's to remain ;
An' may grim misfortune ne'er lay his black paw
On the pow o' my worthy auld freend, Johnnie Waugh.

The Deil's got in the Lasses, O.

AIR—"*Green Grow the Rashes, O*"

Chorus—THE deil's got in the lasses, O !
The deil's got in the lasses, O !
Ilk month or twa Dame Fashion's law.
Aye mak's them unco fashious, O !

Our women-folk are a' gaun daft
Wi' whims an' whigmaleeries, O ;
Their heids are filled sae fu' o' dress
They're spinnin' roun' like peeries, O.
The deil's got in, &c.

Their mithers used to be content
Wi' claes o' their ain spinnin', O ;
Their dochters now maun be arrayed
In purple an' fine linen, O.
The deil's got in, &c.

Wi' chignons, wheels, an' waterfa's,
To mak' them braw and bonnie, O,
They never think to get them a'
It costs a mint o' money, O.
The deil's got in, &c.

Wi' feathers wavin' richt and left,
An' streamers gay and gaudy, O,

To kirk or market now they gang
As grand as ony leddy, O.
    The deil's got in, &c.

Wi' bonnets just like spider's webs
That hang round some auld pillar, O,
They're unco sma', but yet for a',
They cost a heap o' siller, O.
    The deil's got in, &c.

But things will hae to tak' a change,
Or else it's my opinion, O,
Auld maids will soon be found in scores
Throughout the hale Dominion, O.
    The deil's got in, &c.

Sae, lasses, mind what ye're aboot,
If ye intend to marry, O ;
Gae owre your glaikit ways in dress,
Or ye maun single tarry, O.
    The deil's got in, &c,

A Wee Drappie o't.

WHILE we sit here to-night we'll be merry and free,
And as Time passes by still contented we'll be ;
Let the cares of this world for the present be forgot,
While we're a' met together o'er a wee drappie o't.

Chorus—A wee drappie o't, &c,

In our journey through life we must all play our parts,
Then let Love, Truth and Friendship remain in our hearts ;
Let us kindly help each other for to bear our chequered lot,
And at times, when we are happy, hae a wee drappie o't.

Chorus—A wee drappie o't, &c,

Success then to Canada, and honor'd may she be,
May her fame be extended by land and by sea ;
May her commerce thrive and flourish till it's found in ilka
    spot ;
May we aye hae peace and plenty, and a wee drappie o't.

Chorus—A wee drappie o't, &c.

A bumper to Hamilton, we'll pledge her to-night,
May her sons still " Advance " in the cause of Truth and
    Right ;
Here's to a' her bonnie lassies, and may heaven bless their lot,
And send them a' guid husbands, and a wee drappie o't.

Chorus—A wee drappie o't, &c.

Watty Muirhead

A TRUE " Glasco chappie " is Watty Muirhead ;
He's hearty an' happy is Watty Muirhead ;
There's nae better butcher ere killed a beast deid
Than the ane that I sing o', that's Watty Muirhead.
He's up at his wark ere the sun shows its face—
To rowe up his sleeves he ne'er thinks a disgrace ;
He waits on his customers a' day wi' speed,
Baith rich folk an' puir folk like Watty Muirhead.

On Sundays ye'll whiles hear him singing the psalms,
On Mondays he's makin' minced collops or hams ;
If he gies you his word it's as guid as his aith—
Far mair sae than some that gangs roun' in braid claith ;
Throughout the hale kintra he's kent far an' near
As a man that is honest, upright an' sincere ;
If you want a true friend that will help you in need,
There's nae better fellow than Watty Muirhead.

He's no very rich, an' he's no very puir—
" Contented wi' little and happy wi' mair ;"
Tho' he prizes life's comforts, he's no gien to greed,
But social an' kindly is Watty Muirhead.
May his joys a' be doubled, his cares flee awa',
An' still gain respect frae the great an' the sma',
An' lang may it be ere Death nicks his life's thread,
Or tak's frae amang us *our* Watty Muirhead.

Rosa, Dear.

A SOUTHERN DITTY.

AH, ROSA, if you only knew
    The love I bear for you,
I do not think that you would ask
    If Loui still is true ;
For hard had been my fate if love
    Had not dispelled the gloom,
And kept my heart with joys elate,
    And dreams of days to come.
Then do not ask me, Rosa, dear,
    If Loui still be true,
For not a pulse within his heart
    But beats and throbs for you.

You mind when we were very young,
    On Master Green's estate,
How hard I toiled that you might rest
    In noon-day's scorching heat ;
And when our daily task was done,
    And all the field was clear,
Did I not linger still behind
    To woo my Rosa, dear ?
Then do not ask me, Rosa, dear,
    If Loui still is true,
For not a pulse within his heart
    But beats and throbs for you.

But now the curse of slavery's o'er,
 And freedom's goal is won,
Will Rosa join her fate to one
 Whose heart is all her own ?
For well I know you will be true,
 As Loui still hath been ;
O, if the world were all mine own,
 My Rosa would be Queen.
Then do not ask me, Rosa, dear,
 If Loui still is true,
For not a pulse within his heart
 But beats and throbs for you.

The Caledonian.

AIR—" *The Englishman.*"

THERE'S a land where the heather and thistle wave
  Where the foot of a slave ne'er trod,
Where the blue bells bloom o'er her martyrs' grave,
  And hallowed is that sod.
There's a land whose sons are staunch and brave,
  Whose mountains are lofty and grand,
Whose shores are kissed by the blue sea wave,
  And Scotia is that land.
        'Tis an honored place that same proud land,
        The home of the Caledonian.

There's a land whose bards have struck their lyres
  To none but the loftiest strains ;
Whose inspiring tones would call forth fire
  From the dullest coward's veins.
There's a land where noble Wallace fell,
  The first in freedom's van,
Whose name still sounds like a magic spell—
  And Scotia is that land.
        'Tis teeming with heroes that mountain land,
        The home of the Caledonian.

All other lands the palm must yield
  To Scotia's daughters fair ;

And in the tented battle-field
  Her sons are foremost there.
Her tartan-plaided warriors
  Have climbed the steeps of fame ;
Their daring deeds the wide world o'er
  Have earned a deathless name.
        'Tis a nation of heroes—deny it who can—
        The home of the Caledonian.

The Scotsman need not blush to own
  The land that gave him birth,
For her name is known from zone to zone
  As the noblest spot on earth.
Should the foot of a foe e'er dare to tread
  On that little land of the free,
The thistle would raise his stately head,
  Saying, " *You mauna meddle wi' me.*"
        It's a sturdy plant that guards our land,
        The pride of the Caledonian.

The Thirteenth is Ready.

RESPECTFULLY DEDICATED TO THE OFFICERS AND MEN OF THE
13TH BATTALION, HAMILTON.

AIR—"*March of the Cameron Men.*"

THE Thirteenth is ready, whene'er duty calls,
To fight like their fathers of yore ;
Though danger may threaten it never appals
The brave and the loyal of Gore.

I hear their bugles sounding, sounding,
Loud by Ontario's shore,
And the tramp of their footsteps is heard thro'
the vale,
'Tis the march of the heroes of Gore.

The heart of a patriot beats in each breast
As proudly they march to the field ;
They have sworn to fight for their country and Queen,
They may die, but they never will yield !

I hear their bugles sounding, sounding, &c.

To the front was the war-cry that pealed thro' the land,
When the Fenians invaded our shore ;
And *Semper Paratus** was answered by all
Of the brave and the loyal of Gore.

I hear their bugles sounding, sounding, &c.

---

* The motto of the Battalion.

Robert Burns.

AIR—" *Will he no come back again ?* "

WHA o' Robin has nae heard,
  He wha Scotsmen loe sae weel,
Honor'd aye be Scotia's bard—
  Robin was a clever chiel.

     Dear's his fame to us, ye ken,
     Dear's his fame to us, ye ken,
     Scotia's muse by hill an' glen
     Sings his praises o'er again.

Genius shone within his e'e,
  Manliness upon his broo ;
Ithers may hae sung as sweet,
  Nane to Nature sang sae true.

     Dear's his fame to us, ye ken, etc.

Open was his heart an' han',
  Poortith found in him a frien'
Wha like Robin e'er could ban,
  A' things that were fause an' mean.

     Dear's his fame to us, ye ken, etc.

Worth was aye what maist he prized,
  Honesty he made his theme,
Gowd an' tinsel he despised
  If nae merit came wi' them.

> Dear's his fame to us, ye ken, etc.

A' the world has owned his worth—
  Nane his thrawart fate but mourns—
Proud's the wee land in the North,
  O' her minstrel, Robert Burns.

> Dear's his fame to us, ye ken, etc.

A Song for St. Andrew's Day.

How's a' wi' you the nicht, my frién's,
    I'm glad to see you here,
The gatherin' o' the clans, ye ken,
    Takes place but ance a year.
Shame fa' the Scot, where'er he be,
    ·That wadna homage pay
To Scotland and her patron saint,
    Upon his natal day.

Upon this nicht, wi' fond delicht,
    The memory aften turns
To thochts that hae been waukened up
    By Tannahill and Burns;
While listening to their hamely lays,
    They aye bring back to min',
The heather hills, and mountain rills,
    And days o' auld lang syne.

Our auld respectit mither aft
    Looks o'er wi' wistfu' een,
Across the wide Atlantic, to
    Where Canada is seen.
She's unco proud o' a' her sons,
    That walk in honor's way,
And likes to hear their deeds rehears'd,
    Upon St. Andrew's Day.

O, Scotia ! land o' honest men,
   And lassies leal and true,
Though wanderers from thy shore, our hearts
   Will aye return to you.
We'll ne'er forget the land o' cakes
   Where'er we chance to gae,
But meet and sing its praises aye,
   Upon St. Andrew's Day.

Auld Scotia's Roaring Game.

(Respectfully dedicated to the President and Members of the Thistle
Curling Club, Hamilton, Ont.)

Now, Hamilton, haud up your heid ;
    Your bairns may crousley craw ;
At playing o' the channel stane,
    Your callants ding them a'.
The Thistle Club o' Hamilton
    Hae won a glorious name ;
Whaure'er they be, they bear the gree,
    At Scotia's " roaring game."

Auld Scotia's roaring game,
    Auld Scotia's roaring game ;
" The channel stane on icy plain "
    Is Scotia's roaring game.

Their "skips" are clever chiels, I trow,
    And brawly do they ken
The way to lay a " pat-lid" doon
    Or lift it aff again.
Wi' anxious e'e they scan the "tee, "
    Like Generals o' fame,
When, broom in han', they take their stan'
    At Scotia's " roaring game."

Kind-hearted fellows are they a',
    And fu' o' fun and glee ;

A blither set than they ne'er met
   To play around a "tee."
To gen'rous hospitality
   They also can lay claim ;
They've aye a friendly grip for a'
   At Scotia's "roaring game."

Lang may they live to throw a stane,
   And triumph o'er their foes ;
And, victors, dine on " beef and greens,"
   And pree their " Athole brose."
May Hamilton still foremost be
   Upon the scroll o' fame ;
And may her curlers bear the gree
   At Scotia's "roaring game,"

Donald Dinnie,

Donald Dinnie's comin' here,
Donald Dinnie's comin' here ;
Spread the news baith far and near,
That Donald Dinnie's comin' here.

Donald's no like " Heather Jock,"
He has come o' decent folk ;
In his kilts he looks sae braw,
He'll be a credit to us a' ;
Donald though he's big and stoot,
He's nae awkward, ill-faur'd loot ;
In manners he is frank and free,
A brawny, bold atheletc is he.

Donald Dinnie's comin' here,
Donald Dinnie's comin' here ;
Tell the news baith far and near,
That Donald Dinnie's comin' here.

Donald he's a clever chiel,
Can toss the caber like the deil :
At throwin' o' the muckle stane,
He bears the gree whaure'er he's gane :
In ilka thing he tak's in han',
He far surpasses ony man—

A perfect "Crichton" in his ways,
In a' he does an' a' he says.

Donald Dinnie's comin' here,
Donald Dinnie's comin' here ;
Tell the news baith far and near,
That Donald Dinnie's comin' here.

Ye wha lo'e the land o' cakes,
Welcome Donald for its sake ;
Show him by your presence here
That you prize the Thistle dear :
When you hear the piper blaw,
Gather round him ane an' a' ;
Wi' a hearty, rousing cheer,
Welcome Donald Dinnie here.

Donald Dinnie's comin' here,
Donald Dinnie's comin here ;
Tell the news baith far and near,
That Donald Dinnie's comin' here.

The Laird o' the "Station Hotel." *

Ye'll a' hae heard tell o' the Laird o' Cockpen,
And o' auld Dugal Paul, and o' mony sic men ;
But I'll sing ye o' ane that ye a' ken yoursel',
It's the cantie wee laird o' the Station Hotel.

Noo Davie's a man that's leal-hearted and true,
And he cares na a bodle what ither folk do,
Ye'll aye find him honest and upricht himsel',
And a' his bit pride is the Station Hotel.

His heart it is big tho' his stature be sma',
He's a pouch where he keeps a bit "shillin' or twa,"
If he meets wi' a frien' he aye uses him well,
It's the rule o' the house, at the Station Hotel.

But he's no ane o' them that's conceited or vain,
An' he'll ne'er wrang a man for the sake o' his gain,
But in gude social friendship there's nane can excel
The cantie wee laird o' the Station Hotel.

If you happen to stap in some nicht in the gloamin',
He'll sing ye the "Sorrows o' Waggletail's Woman,"
How he fed her on crowdie, an' broo an' lang kail,
She'd hae got better board at the Station Hotel.

Mr. David Henderson, better known by the sobriquet of "Wee Davie."

If yere fash'd wi' the blues, or get dung o'er with care,
Or oppressed wi' the things o' this warl' o'er sair,
An' ye want to get rid o' them a' for a spell,
Just tak a stap down to the Station Hotel.

Ye can ha'e a douce crack, ye can hear a guid sang,
The nicht passes by, and ye ne'er think it lang.
It seems but a jiffy, frae nine until twel'
When ye crack wi' the laird o' the Station Hotel.

He is always as blythe as a body can be,
He's aye open-hearted aff-handed and free,
And for raising a splore he's a host in himsel',
He's the cock o' the walk at the Station Hotel.

Sae here's to ye, Dave, may ye lang wag yer pow,
An' gang daunering about, just as ye're doing now,
And may cauld, thowless sorrow or poverty snell,
Ne'er come in at the door o' your Station Hotel.

An' in years after this, when ye're laid in the mools,
An' the earth happit o'er ye wi' spades, and wi' shools,
May ye gang up aboon, wi' guid fellows to dwell,
When ye're dune wi' the warl' an' the Station Hotel.

A Song, a Song for Canada.

"DEDICATED TO THE ROYAL CANADIAN SOCIETY OF GRIMSBY."

A SONG, a song for Canada,
   The brightest and the best
Of all the lands that lie within
   The borders of the West.
There Nature spreads her choicest gifts
   Throughout her wide domain—
Then sing the praise of Canada,
   Again and yet again.

A song, a song for Canada—
   The star of empire gleams
On that proud land of forests grand,
   Of rivers, lakes and streams.

Her boundless realms stretch far and wide,
   And reach from sea to sea ;
Her fields are filled with waving grain,
   Her woods with melody.
Her sons are brave, her daughters pure,
   Her honor bears no stain—
Then sing the praise of Canada,
   Again and yet again.

A song, a song for Canada—
   The star of empire gleams

On that proud land of forests grand,
Of rivers lakes and streams.

Though Britain's bards with one accord
Old England's praises swell,
Give me the land where gallant Brock
And brave Tecumseh fell ;
For freedom dwells within its dells
And there it will remain—
Then sing the praise of Canada,
Again and yet again.

A song, a song for Canada—
The star of empire gleams
On that proud land of forests grand,
Of rivers, lakes and streams.

LOCAL PIECES.

A City Lyric.

"DEDICATED TO THE MAYOR AND MEMBERS OF THE CORPORATION
OF THE CITY OF HAMILTON."

Awake the snorting citizens with the bell, or else the devil will make a grandsire
of some of you.—*Shakspeare—Latest edition.*

THERE's a town in auld Scotland they ca' it Dunkeld,
Whaur they knocked down the steeple and fuddled the bell;
And I think the folks here would be doing what's right,
If they pulled down our bell and our belfry some night.

Our bell's little else but a tumblin'-tam—
In its very best days it was naught but a sham ;
The place where it hangs in would do very weel
For an auld huckster's hen-coop or fisherman's creel.

It's a shame and disgrace to our city, I trow,
That the auld crazy structure we dinna renew ;
Some ane will be killed yet, o' that ye'll hear tell,
On some dark stormy night when they're ringing the bell.

Our policemen a' are afraid for to ring it—
It jiggles and joggles whenever they swing it ;

When they're pulling the rope they are standing in dreed
That the hale fabrication will fa' on their heid.

It's of nae use of asking our Councillors ava
For to get it repaired till it happens to fa';
They need a' the siller aye now and again,
To bring out some new-fangled schemes o' their ain.

The de'il tak' them a', not forgetting the Mayor,
I think whiles mysel' that they dinna act fair;
When they want to raise money—frae door unto door,
They send round Tam Tindill and Peter Balfour.

I'll no misca' them when their duty they do—
I believe in my saul they are honest and true;
But if things were weel guided 'mang them for a spell,
They might soon raise enough for a steeple and bell.

Is there nane o' our merchants got siller at a'
Is there nae Geordie Peabodys 'mang them ava?
If there is, it is time they cam' out o' their shell,
And help us to get a new steeple and bell.

My blessing on him, aye, wha led the way first,
That gave us a fountain to slaken our thirst;
His name will be honor'd—I wish that there were
A few more amang us like Archibald Kerr.

There are chances for ithers to get up their name—
We're wanting a town-clock—wha'll give us that same?
If our Council had ony respect for itsel',
We would ne'er need their help for a steeple or bell.

Is there nane o' our Aldermen daur tak' the lead ?
Is there nane will rise up and with eloquence plead ?
Is there nane that with glory would cover himsel',
By trying to get us a steeple and bell ?

Up, Murison, up on your feet ; raise your hand—
Let the Mayor and the rest of them all understand,
When election day comes we will bid them farewell,
If they dinna provide us a steeple and bell.

Wha's to be our Mayor now?

AIR—"*Castles in the Air.*"

WHA's to be our Mayor now?
Wha's to be our Mayor?
Wha's to be the honor'd man will fill our civic chair?
Geordie Mills and Charlton hae filled it weel before,
And gin we ne'er get waur than them our troubles will be o'er.
I'm finding faut wi' naebody, but this I here declare,
I'd like to see a worthy man get in to be our Mayor.

Wha's to be our Mayor now?
Wha's to be our Mayor?
Wha is puin' at the wires to fill our civic chair?
Wlll it be O'Reilly, or will it Waddell be?
Or aiblins Johnnie Eastwood, the chief amang the three?
There's Lister, Peirce, and Chisholm, too, a' men that's fair
    and square,
But wha's amang us that can tell which o' them will be Mayor?

Wha's to be our Mayor now?
Wha's to be our Mayor?
Wha's to be the lucky man to fill our civic chair?
McCarty or Fitzpatrick would answer vera weel,
Or Johnnie I. Mackenzie, for he's a clever chiel;

Guid gear's row'd up in bundles sma', there's nocht o' him to
   spare,
I think mysel' we might hae waur than Johnnie for our Mayor.

But now ye fifteen "chosen ones" ye soon will take your
   place,
Ye've got the honors that ye sought, ne'er bring them to
   disgrace ;
Aye hae the city's weal at heart—act just by great and sma'
And if ye dinna do what's richt, the deevil tak' ye a' ;
Reduce our taxes, if you can, let that be your first care,
And gie' us cause to bless ye a', and him you choose for Mayor.

The City Park.

TRUTHFUL L. X. & R. TO THE EDITOR—

"A little nonsense, now and then,
Is relished by the wisest men."

WE want a nice park for the city,
  There's few that will say against that ;
But surely it is a great pity
  A decent one can't be got at
Without going out to the township of Barton before we can
    " squat."

It's all very well for those people
  Who own fine " turn-outs " and fast nags,
And wear hats as high as a steeple
  And live on their rich money-bags ;
But what's to become of the *blouses* who can't drive down
    there in their drags ?

Must they " waddle " down to the race-course,
  And carry the " kids " in their arms,
While the sun pours his rays down in great force
  And freckles and spoils all their charms,
Creating a row and a discord that equal War's wildest alarms.

George H. Mills, the dauntless, where are you ?
  Come forward, and fight like a man ;

Be a " brick," don't let any one scare you,
    But stick like a burr to your plan.
Go in on your muscle, my Trojan, and keep things correct—
    if you can.

Our Aldermen, somehow or other,
    Don't do things exactly just right;
They cause us a good deal of bother,
    (I don't say they ever get *tight*)
But mix up things so that our taxes are getting as *high* as a
    kite.

I have heard of a wind that's unstable,
    That's not good for man nor for beast ;
I have read—but it must be a fable—
    That the wise men all come from the East,
To say so of those in our city, would seem like a big joke
    at least.

Why the deuce did they not purchase Dundurn,
    When it could have been bought for a song?
When we wanted to do them a good turn,
    They thought we were all in the wrong—
And some of them gave their opinion in words emphasized
    pretty strong.

I know that in Summer it's pleasant
    (When Sol has ta'en out his degrees)
To a man, whether peer or a peasant,
    To rest in the shade 'neath the trees,
With Susan Jane sitting beside him, and list to the murmur
    of bees.

But he who would travel to sun-rise
  To find out a spot to keep cool,
Must have had some gold-dust thrown in his eyes,
  Or else he must be a born fool;
Well, I wont say he's foolish, but surely he didn't learn much
  while at school.

Let us have a good park—we won't rue it—
  But then, let it be in a place
Where we'll all have a chance to get to it,
  As it should be in every such case;
The men who get this excel Darwin and do far more good
  to their race.

Sam Lover—and he was no churl,
  And none will deny he knew best,
When he said " there's no *land* in the world
  Like the *land* of the beautiful West."
Then get us a park in the West end, and set this vexed
  question at rest!

The Woman in Black.

THE ghosts—long ago—used to dress in pure white,
  Now they're got on a different track,—
For the Hamilton Ghost seems to take a delight
  To stroll 'round the city in black.

Pat Duffy, who saw her in Corktown last night,
  Has been heard to-day telling his friend
That she stood seven feet and nine inches in height,
  And wore a large Grecian Bend.

A " Peeler," who met her, turned blue with affright,
  And in terror he clung to a post ;
His hair (once a carroty red) has turned white,
  Since the moment he looked on the ghost.

Her appearance was frightful to gaze on, he said,—
  It filled him with horror complete ;
For she looked unlike anything, living or dead,
  That ever he'd seen on his beat.

Her breath seemed as hot as a furnace ; besides,
  It smelt strongly of sulphur and gin,
Two horns (a yard long) stuck straight out of her head,
  And her hoofs made great clatter and din.

Her air was majestic, and terribly grand,
  As she passed, muffled up in her veil ;

A bottle of "ruin" she held in each hand,
And she uttered a low, plaintive wail :

" ' There is rest for the weary,' but no rest for me ;
I cannot find rest if I try,—
Three months and three days I have been on the spree ;
(Mr. Mueller, ' How's that for high ?')

" I have mixed in the world, both with ' spirits' and men,—
Once more with the spirits I'll go."
She stopped, took a sniff of the " ruin," and then
She popped into a cellar below.

He could hear her again, crying out from her den—
" To-night you will see me no more ;
But I'll meet with you Saturday evening at ten,
By the fountain that stands in the Gore."

Some people that passed there this morning at two,
Found the " Peeler " still glued to his post ;
He told them this yarn I have been telling you—
And that's the last news from the Ghost !

POEMS AND SONGS.

254

Advertise.

"A man's business increases in ratio according to the amount of advertising that he does."—*Horace Greeley*.

LET dogs delight to bark and bite,
Let statesmen tell us wrong is right,
Let lawyer loons swear black is white—
    As sometimes they will do,—
And "local editors" get tight,
    For 'tis their nature too.

Let poets when they're making rhyme,
Rush from ridiculous to sublime ;
Let railroad trains be run on time,
    (Something not always done),
And maidens marry in their prime
    (Say when they're twenty-one.)

Let those whose hearts are filled with fears,
Retire to more congenial spheres,
And leave us in this "vale of tears"
    To toil and work away,
Rejoicing that the coming years
    Will bring "nine hours a day."

Let parsons preach and scribblers scrawl,—
The world is wide, there's room for all ;

Let justice—at the City Hall—
　Unerringly be done ;
Yea, even though the heavens fall
　On this our Hamilton.

Let those who wealth and power would find,
No longer try to " go it blind ;"
Or in the race they'll lag behind
　And lose the wished for prize ;
Unless they always bear in mind,
　Their " Biz " to ADVERTISE.

That man will be held up to scorn
By generations yet unborn,
Who does not daily " blow his horn "
　Throughout the Public Press.
Burns said that " man was made to mourn."
　It is not so, I guess.

If man had only sense to see,
The true road to prosperity,
Then printer's ink would flow more free,
　And each and every one
Would flourish like a green bay tree
　That's basking in the sun.

The moral of all this is plain—
That he who is not quite insane,
In idleness will not remain
　While goods lie on his shelf ;
But ADVERTISE, then wealth he'll gain ;—
　You know how it is yourself.

www.ingramcontent.com/pod-product-compliance
Lightning Source LLC
Chambersburg PA
CBHW030359270326
41926CB00009B/1188